Ministry Greenhouse

Ministry Greenhouse

Cultivating Environments for
Practical Learning

George M. Hillman, Jr.

THE
ALBAN
INSTITUTE
Herndon, Virginia
www.alban.org

The Alban Institute
2121 Cooperative Way, Suite 100
Herndon, VA 20171

Scripture quotations, unless otherwise noted, are from The Holy Bible, English Standard Version®, copyright © 2001 by Crossway Bibles, a publishing ministry of Good News Publishers. Used by permission. All rights reserved.

Scripture quotations noted as NLT are from the Holy Bible, New Living Translation, copyright © 1996. Used by permission of Tyndale House Publishers, Inc., Wheaton, IL 60189. All rights reserved.

Cover design by Signal Hill.

Library of Congress Cataloging-in-Publication Data

Hillman, George M.
 Ministry greenhouse : cultivating environments for practical learning / George M. Hillman, Jr.
    p. cm.
 Includes bibliographical references (p.   ).
 ISBN 978-1-56699-360-9
 1. Pastoral theology—Fieldwork. 2. Internship programs. 3. Clergy—Training of. 4. Christian leadership. I. Title.

 BV4164.5.H55 2008
 253.071'55—dc22
                        2008004456

        12   11   10   09   08   VP   1   2   3   4   5

Contents

Preface   vii

Acknowledgments   xi

Chapter 1   Why Internships?   1

Chapter 2   What Is God Calling You to Do?   11

Chapter 3   What Are the Ingredients for a   37
             Healthy Internship?

Chapter 4   What Are the Goals for Your   69
             Internship?

Chapter 5   What Did You Learn during   91
             Your Internship?

Epilogue   Playing in the Dirt   121

Appendix A   Recommended Resources   125

Appendix B   General Ministry Leadership   127
             Competencies

Appendix C   Specific Ministry Skill Competencies   131

Appendix D   Sample Goals   139

Notes   147

Bibliography   157

Preface

I have the wonderful pleasure of being the "internship guy" on a seminary campus. Talking to students on a daily basis about God's movement in their lives is my privilege. When I have these conversations, I am reminded of myself at their age, considering many of the same questions, uncertainties, and anticipations. This book is an attempt to put in writing what I have been telling students in my office for years. I have written this book with these ministry students in mind.

Terms I Use

Instead of using a sterile "the student" or "the intern" to talk about the process of setting up and fulfilling a college or seminary internship, my intent is to make this book approachable and, therefore, I use the more personal *you* when addressing the reader because I assume the primary reader is a college or seminary student. If you are an internship mentor, supervisor, coach, or layperson reading this book, just substitute the student's name for *you* throughout the book and things should make sense.

Different schools use different terms for the person who works with the intern during an internship. Some schools use the word *mentor*. Other schools use the word *supervisor* or *coach*. I have chosen the word *mentor* because I think it communicates a warmer dynamic than *supervisor* or *coach*. What takes place in an internship is more than an employee and employer relationship. Real mentoring (discussed in detail later in this book) is the goal. Throughout the book, please substitute your school's term for this person as necessary.

Throughout *Ministry Greenhouse*, I speak about the relationship between the mentor and the student. In choosing to use the term *mentor* almost exclusively for clarity's sake, I do not want to exclude others who may be involved in the internship process. Depending on the setting and the requirements, you as a student intern may have a lay committee or an advisory council involved in the process. For example, at Dallas Theological Seminary where I work, we ask students to have four "ministry consultants" in addition to their mentor. The number and role of these people vary greatly depending on the school and the denomination. In those settings where such a group is required, a group of lay people (usually but not always) works alongside the on-site mentor in providing feedback, guidance, assessment, and prayer support throughout the internship. If a member of such a supervisory group is reading this book, he or she will find that many of the items specifically addressed to the mentor can easily be applied to a supervisory group member. Although supervisory group members may not have as much time with the intern as the mentor does or will, they are still valuable members of the team.

A final note about word choice throughout the book: While *internship* is the preferred term at Dallas Theological Seminary, I know that every school uses a different term—field education, practicum, residency, apprenticeship, practical training, pastoral training, and so on. I also know that the duration of these learning experiences varies—from five hours a week in a local setting to a summer immersion experience to a yearlong residency. So when you read *internship*, substitute the word on your campus that refers to the ministerial training that takes place in the field instead of in the classroom.

My Hope for You

While much of the material in this book comes from my experiences at Dallas Theological Seminary, I believe it is transferable to any college or seminary setting. Although I serve at a nondenominational evangelical seminary, I have aimed to write this book so that it can be used as a resource across the spectrum of theological schools and denominational traditions. Throughout the book I note where denominational traditions may differ from one to another. However, no matter the school or the internship site, the basics of internships are the same.

Keeping in mind my mantra that students need to engage the world outside of the classroom more, I have tried to keep the book as brief as possible without sacrificing depth. The last thing I want is for you to be locked up in your room reading another book about how you need to be doing ministry. My hope is that every reader will find this book a quick and informative read.

> And so, from the day we heard, we have not ceased to pray for you, asking that you may be filled with the knowledge of his will in all spiritual wisdom and understanding, so as to walk in a manner worthy of the Lord, fully pleasing to him, bearing fruit in every good work and increasing in the knowledge of God. May you be strengthened with all power, according to his glorious might, for all endurance and patience with joy, giving thanks to the Father, who has qualified you to share in the inheritance of the saints in light.
>
> —Colossians 1:9-12

Acknowledgments

In writing this book, I have been reminded of how blessed I am to work at Dallas Theological Seminary. I am thankful to the entire staff of the Howard G. Hendricks Center for Christian Leadership for their constant support and encouragement, particularly Howard Hendricks, Andy Seidel, Dave Kanne, Paul Pettit, Pam Cole, Erin Stambaugh, Terry Hebert, Dipa Hart, and Pauline Montgomery. Working with this group of godly servant leaders is a privilege.

I also extend my gratitude to Aubrey Malphurs of Dallas Theological Seminary for taking a chance on me, a young "outsider." I have never enjoyed a job more. I have always appreciated his friendship, his confidence in me, and his words of wisdom.

In the journey of writing my first book, my editor Rochelle Melander and the staff at the Alban Institute have been a joy to work with. Rochelle stretched me to take a simple structure that I have been using with our students and pushed me to create a broader work. Her words were well-timed and on target, and I thank her for the coaching.

Finally, I express my love to the two women of my life: my wife, Jana, and my daughter, Katherine. The greatest joys in my life have been spent with the two of them.

CHAPTER 1

Why Internships?

ONE REASON I AM PASSIONATE ABOUT THE VALUE OF internships is that my own seminary internship played such an important role in my life. I came to seminary after working for a nonprofit organization for a few months following college. Reflecting on that experience, I realize that during the first year of my seminary studies I did not fully engage my academic pursuits.

I can think of several reasons for my distraction. I was fresh out of college and enjoying some of the freedom of living in a big city. I was newly married (my wife and I got married two weekends after graduating college together). I was not sure what God was doing in my life at the time or what my ministry direction should be. As a result of these and other factors, I floated through my first year or so of seminary with little focus.

However, all of that changed during my second year of seminary. With the prospects of an internship looming ahead of me, I began to investigate my options. Although later I recognized God's providence, I participated, on what I considered a whim, in a campus interview for an internship working with college students in Georgia. I had enjoyed my own college experience and especially the ministry exposure I received at my college church. Therefore, I thought I would check things out with this interview to learn about internships in general. In my mind I did not actually intend to follow through on this opportunity, and I sure was not going to move to another state to do my internship. As a native Texas boy, I never saw myself moving to the land of sweet tea and pork barbeque.

Well, as you have probably guessed, God had other plans. The interview was a fantastic experience and I was offered an internship working with college students at the University of Georgia. My wife and I had no hesitation in the move. But little did we know that what was supposed to have been a nine-month internship with this campus ministry would turn into more than six years of ministry to college students on that campus. This Texas boy fell in love with Georgia. Moreover, in the stretching my internship allowed, I discovered my passion for working with students in an academic setting. While my campus setting has changed with my move from a large state university to a nondenominational seminary, my passion has remained. As the kick start for recalibrating my ministry, the internship in Georgia served as a truly life-altering season in my life, in my family's life, and for my ministry direction.

Internships Balance Theological Education

Schools of theological education see one of their purposes as leadership development, yet many critics would say that the modern Bible college or seminary is failing to train leaders of the twenty-first century. Some church leaders and scholars would go so far as to say that many present-day theological education institutions likely will not survive long into the twenty-first century, due in part to this perceived lack of leadership development in the schools' graduates. As a result, many of the largest churches in America no longer seek candidates from seminaries to fill job openings, instead opting to hire from within, developing nontraditional theological training and on-the-job training opportunities.

For most of the last fifty years, theologians, pastors, and congregations have debated the purpose of theological education institutions. At the heart of the debate is one question: is the purpose of the Bible college or seminary to train theologians or to train practitioners? Indeed, higher education as a whole questions the relationship between theoretical knowledge and practical experience. Is the purpose of formal education to help the student think critically or function practically?

Theological   Ministry
Equipping   How-To

Figure 1.1. Balance in Theological Education

On one side of the debate about theological education are those who believe the role of Bible colleges and seminaries is to *theologically equip* students to think biblically and critically rather than simply to help them develop particular pastoral skills. With respect to leadership development, proponents of this view contend that theological education needs to focus on creating theologically minded students and to encourage students to learn the practical aspects of ministry in other venues. These venues include both secular and religious settings. In addition, they argue that the primary location for leadership development is the local church rather than the formal classroom.

Scholars on the other side of the theological education debate see the role of these schools as educating a professional church leader in *ministry how-tos*. This debate has primarily taken place at the grassroots level where a vocal coalition of church leaders has voiced its concern that the training received by ministers-to-be in Bible colleges and seminaries is not applicable to the real world. These church leaders strongly believe that theological education needs to make a more concerted effort to educate future leaders who can lead both inside and outside the local church. Some critics have gone so far as to call for and even create their own church-based theological education, bypassing accredited seminaries entirely. An unfortunate and occasional result of this debate has been a damaged relationship between the churches that develop these programs and particular theological schools.

In reality, the Bible college or seminary has to do both the practical application and the theological equipping for ministry. Part of the role of theological education is to prepare students to think biblically and critically. Too much ministry that takes place today lacks strong theological roots. At the same time, the theological school needs to prepare students like you to take your vast theological knowledge from the classroom and soundly engage in ministry in a variety of modern contexts.

Nevertheless, the school cannot do it all; it can only take you so far. Internships serve as a link between theory and practice. Instead of learning only in the isolation of the classroom, an internship supports your learning within the community of faith as you minister in a specific context and reflect on that experience.

Internships Are Vital to Leadership Development

Many Bible colleges, seminaries, and professional organizations call their internship programs "field education" because education takes place literally in the "field" of service. An internship is not busy work or cheap labor but is instead a fundamental element to your intentional development as a future leader. A great internship experience can place you in an environment where God can work through you in the lives of other people and, more important, where God can work in your own life to develop calling, character, and competencies.

The Association of Theological Schools (ATS) is the agency that accredits more than two-hundred-fifty theological schools in the United States and Canada. In its accrediting process, ATS produces standards that quantify requirements related to theological field education, including scholarship, curriculum, faculty standards, and individual degree plans. In its 2002 report, ATS states that 94.6 percent of all masters-level students had some type of internship or field education experience during their academic career. In surveying graduating ministry students, ATS reports that 82.9 percent of all graduating masters-level students found their internship experience important for their development. These graduating ministry student respondents said the internship experience improved their pastoral skills, helped them better understand their strengths and weaknesses, instilled more self-confidence in them, and provided them with greater vocational clarity.[1]

Formal education, observation of others, and real-world experience all play a part in leadership development. Generally, the more practical the lessons you need to learn, the more the educational experience needs to be integrated into real life through field-based educational and personalized instruction.

Much of the practical instruction that a minister needs is best learned on the job.

As the leadership laboratory of ministry, congregations and other ministry settings are vital collaborators with academia in developing leaders. Understanding organizational culture, learning leadership and management skills, sharpening people skills, identifying personal strengths and assets, and identifying potential areas of character downfall are all practical lessons learned in an internship.

Educators see internships as helping to overcome the class-room teacher's inability to create real-world learning experiences in the formal classroom setting. If an internship does not work out for a student or for an organization, it is often because this real-world educational element of the internship has been forgotten in the busyness of serving. However, when the school combines its formal education with mentoring and the practical lessons of internship, true leadership development can take place.

The academics of theological education help lay the foundation for a biblical worldview and provide the basic understanding of the ministry trade, but the theoretical needs to be integrated with the practical in the leadership laboratory in the field. God called you to school to learn, but a school's values and curriculum need to reflect this balance between theory and practice. When Bible colleges and seminaries collaborate with the local church and ministry organizations to develop the next generation of leaders, they cultivate leaders who are sound doctrinally and practically.

Leadership Development Needs a Greenhouse

While this book has absolutely nothing to do with flowers or vegetables, its title, *Ministry Greenhouse*, is not a mistake. Like a greenhouse, this book is all about growth. Let me explain.

The word *seminary* comes from a Middle English word meaning "seed plot," "seedbed," or "nursery." The Middle English word, in turn, comes from the Latin word *seminarium*, with the Latin root word *semin* or "seed." Seminary is technically a place or an environment in which something is developed or nurtured.[2]

So what does an agricultural greenhouse do? While greenhouses have existed in some form since Roman times, the modern greenhouse came into existence in the 1800s as a way for Europeans to grow exotic plants. Modern greenhouses are built of glass or plastic, using energy from the sun to warm the plants and the soil inside the greenhouse. The roof and walls retain the air warmed by the sun.

Greenhouses guard plants from the cold, protect plants from dust storms and blizzards, and help keep out pests. This controlled environment can even be adapted to the needs of particular plants. Light and temperature control allow greenhouses to turn even wasteland into arable land.

In some cases, the plants grown inside a greenhouse might stay inside the safe confines of the greenhouse for their entire existence. In other cases, the greenhouse is used as a controlled environment in which to start seedlings until they are able to thrive on their own in the outside world, perhaps once the weather warms up. Although the environment inside the greenhouse is not perfect, a farmer or a gardener using a greenhouse can control the temperature, light, and moisture inside the structure and therefore create the best possible environment for successful growth. In agriculture, the outcome cannot be guaranteed, but a farmer or a gardener can definitely stack the deck in his or her favor.

How interesting it is that the word to describe what goes on at a school that prepares men and women for ministry leadership comes from the world of agriculture. A seminary, a seed plot, when it is working properly, creates an environment where the Holy Spirit can work in your life and the lives of other future ministry leaders: a safe environment to ask questions, a safe environment to stretch your mind and heart, a safe environment to be molded.

Jesus lived in an agrarian society and often used the language of farming in his parables. For example: And [Jesus] said, "The kingdom of God is as if a man should scatter seed on the ground. He sleeps and rises night and day, and the seed sprouts and grows; he knows not how. The earth produces by itself, first the blade, then the ear, then the full grain in the ear. But when the grain is ripe, at once he puts in the sickle, because the harvest has come" (Mark 4:26-29). I think one of the reasons (besides wanting to connect with the audience on their terms) Jesus used an agricultural motif for some of his parables is because plant growth is beyond human control.

I know this lack of control firsthand. Mowing my lawn is one of the simple pleasures I delight in. I actually look forward to walking behind my lawnmower on Saturday mornings, enjoying the Texas summer before the temperatures get too high later in the day. Nevertheless, while I love to mow, I have come to dread the fickleness of my lawn. For example, just when I get rid of all of the clover in my lawn, the dandelions appear. Alternatively, just when I think I have my watering routine figured out, I start to see brown patches of grass from too little water. As any homeowner will tell you, the battle of the yard is never ending.

Having the perfect lawn will always be an elusive dream; the only thing I can do is create an environment where my Bermuda grass can grow. I have no guarantees, but if I have the right amount of water, nutrients, and pest control, I can create an atmosphere for success. I cannot force my lawn to prosper. All I can do is create the growing environment, then watch and wait.

Agriculture is in some ways a mystery, just as spiritual growth is in some ways a mystery. While church leaders and educators can develop programs and systems to try to force or automate spiritual growth, the Holy Spirit does not work that way. In our own lives, the secret is to place ourselves in an environment where the Holy Spirit can work. Similarly, educators, pastors, organization leaders, and lay leaders—those who develop future leaders—have the job of creating an environment where the same transformational process can begin for other people.

The role of a college or seminary is not to force you to grow mentally, emotionally, physically, and spiritually. Rather, the role of the school is to create a learning environment where you are more likely to enjoy success. Moreover, as we have seen in this chapter, an internship is one of the best possible learning environments in which you can place yourself.

Are You Ready to Grow?

This chapter is, I admit, a bit theoretical. The rest of the book, however, is practical. My question for you as we begin this journey together is, why are you in school? Most likely it is because you sense God at work in your life in some meaningful way. In the next chapter, I explore how you can hear the call of God in your life. So if you are ready to grow, let's get started.

Questions for Reflection

1. Why did you come to school in the first place? What is the specific reason you chose your particular school or degree plan?
2. What type of learning—from books, the formal classroom setting, conversation, or practice—do you find most valuable? What growth have you experienced from each type of learning?

3. If you have participated in an internship before, was it a good or a bad experience? If the experience was good, what were the factors that made it good? If the experience was bad, what could have been changed to make it better?

4. In your new internship, what are you hoping to accomplish?

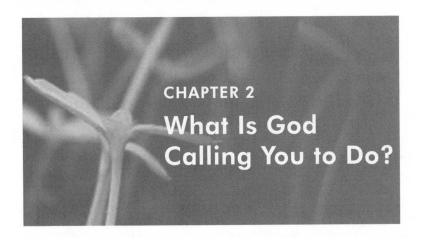

CHAPTER 2

What Is God Calling You to Do?

MINISTRY STUDENTS COME TO SCHOOL FOR A BROAD assortment of reasons and with a wide spectrum of ministry experience. You can probably change the fictitious names in the illustrations below and find most of these students on your Bible college or seminary campus:

- Maria, a high school student, has been an active partici-pant in her church's student ministry. With graduation approaching, some of her friends and family members are now asking her, "Have you ever felt called to ministry?"
- John is a missionary in his fifties who is coming to school to retool for the global mission field and to receive the necessary training to start a Bible college back in another country.
- Susan is in her early twenties and recently graduated from college. Although she is not clear about her future ministry, she knows that God has called her to seminary and is trusting God's direction for the next step.
- Frank is a retired career military man who has al-ways dreamed of going to Bible college for personal enrichment.

- Ann is in her forties and has been a lay leader in her church's women's ministry for many years. With the last of her kids finally in college, Ann is able to seriously consider a paid pastoral position at her local church.
- Bob and Jane are newlyweds who have a passionate interest in Eastern Europe and are considering serving in the global mission field upon graduation.
- Mike became a Christian three years ago after becoming involved in his church's men's ministry. Wanting to learn even more about the Bible, Mike has enrolled in night classes at Bible college.
- Kate is a dynamic leader who has been working as a youth minister while in college. For her, seminary seemed like the natural next step.

From the variety of backgrounds and interests illustrated above, you can see that one size does not fit all when it comes to theological education in general and each student's internship goals in particular. Students not only come to campus with a variety of backgrounds, but they also enjoy a virtual cornucopia of vocational ministry opportunities. Instead of limiting yourself to pulpit ministry or foreign missions, you can consider endless possibilities for ministry in this new millennium. At your seminary or Bible college, future Internet apologetics Web masters, evangelistic rap artists, Christian screenwriters, and biblical researchers now sit in class side by side with the traditional preachers and missionaries. Each has come to school for very different reasons.

Called to Purpose and Meaning

In the opening paragraph of his book *The Call*, theologian and social commentator Os Guinness lays out the following challenge: "Are you looking for purpose in life? For a purpose big enough to absorb every ounce of your attention, deep enough to plumb every mystery of your passions, and lasting enough to inspire you to your last breath?"[1] Guinness goes on to describe the inward longing to find purpose in life, a purpose "bigger than ourselves." He concludes that only the call of God can ever fulfill this longing, describing *calling* as "the truth that God calls us to himself so decisively that everything we are, everything we do, and everything we have is invested with a special devotion, dynamism, and direction lived out as a response to his summons and service."[2]

Many of us come to a point where we decide to examine seriously our strengths, personality, values, and passions; a point where we carefully examine our uniqueness and how God has wired us. We begin to contemplate how God is calling us to engage people and contexts around us, loving people as God would have them loved.

Regrettably, we live in what some theologians call a "post-vocational" or "callingless" world. In such a world, jobs are just paychecks, relationships are random and unconnected, and deeper meaning in life is missing. However, when we recover a biblical sense of vocation or calling, when we live our lives with an understanding that our lives have purpose and meaning, then the everyday becomes holy.

Our calling or vocation has two aspects: a *primary* calling and *functional* callings. Our primary calling is to a living and dynamic relationship with God. Our functional callings are acts of loving service to others.

Your Primary Calling to God

Throughout Scripture, the chief concern is always God calling people into a relationship with God and to a life of holiness.

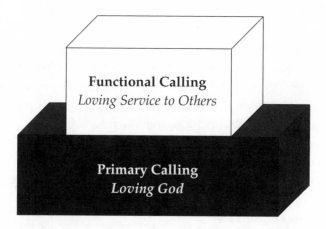

Figure 2.1. Primary Calling and Functional Callings

Your primary calling serves as the umbrella under which you function as a believer. You are called first and foremost to God and not only to a role, a career, or a location.

The biblical writers describe a person's calling almost exclusively in terms of being called to love God and to live a life reflecting that love. Consider some of the following examples where the word *call* is specifically used in the New Testament:

- Called to belong to Jesus Christ (Rom. 1:5-7)
- Called to be conformed to the image of Christ (Rom. 8:28-30)
- Called to be saints and to be in the fellowship of Christ (1 Cor. 1:2)
- Called to live in hope (Eph. 1:18)
- Called to walk in a worthy manner (Eph. 4:1)
- Called to the one hope (Eph. 4:4)
- Called to live in God's glory (1 Thess. 2:12; 2 Thess. 2:14)
- Called to live in holiness (1 Thess. 4:7; 2 Tim. 1:8-9)

- Called to eternal life (1 Tim. 6:12)
- Called to experience God's marvelous light (1 Pet. 2:9)
- Called to eternal glory in Christ (1 Pet. 5:10)
- Called to God's glory and excellence (2 Pet. 1:3)

Even this quick "swim" through the Bible shows that God's primary interest in your life is who you are as an individual and your relationship with God, not primarily what you do as a career.

Unfortunately, most of us naturally gravitate to doing versus being. Especially in a North American context, we jump to thinking about employment or marriage when we speak of the call of God or the will of God. What do you do for a living? What is your major in college? Are you married? We hear those questions on a daily basis—manifestations of North American culture's practical and pragmatic orientation. Added to this, the idea that what a person does to earn a living is a true measure of the person is inbred in our culture.[3] While these things are important, these things do not entirely define who a person is. The concept of calling in the New Testament is always focused on loving God and living a life that reflects that love, not merely on occupation or location or marriage. God wants you to seek him, not only his services. God wants your heart.

Your Functional Callings in Service to Others

In addition to your primary calling to God, you are called to be a Christian in particular social locations. The dimensions of your calling include the following:

- How you act in your immediate and extended families
- How you serve your neighbors

- How you function in the local church
- How you serve the greater society in stewardship and mission
- How you spend your time in work
- How you spend your time in rest

Various functional calls, then, are how you lovingly live out your primary calling to God in daily life among people. In fact, living out your primary calling in the particulars of your life transforms the spheres of your life into functional callings. As responses to God's calling on your life, your functional callings matter as well.[4]

The foundation for the Christian walk is laid with the paving stones of increasing love and devotion to God *and* loving service to others. This is exactly what Jesus meant in his response to the question of priority: "And one of the scribes came up and heard them disputing with one another, and seeing that he answered them well, asked [Jesus], 'Which commandment is the most important of all?' Jesus answered, 'The most important is, "Hear, O Israel: The Lord our God, the Lord is one. And you shall love the Lord your God with all your heart and with all your soul and with all your mind and with all your strength." The second is this: "You shall love your neighbor as yourself." There is no other commandment greater than these'" (Mark 12:28-31). So ask yourself, "Am I loving God and am I loving others?"

Under the umbrella of your primary calling to salvation and sanctification, your functional callings are the ways in which you love and serve others. Loving acts are not attempts to earn favor with God; that is God's work of grace in your life. But with an understanding that love comes out of the grace you receive, loving others as God would love them becomes the benchmark of whether you are fulfilling your functional callings.

Opportunities to love others are all around. Reformation leader Martin Luther believed, "Reflect on your condition, and you will find enough good works to do if you would lead a godly life. Every calling has its own duties, so that we need not inquire for others outside of our station."[5] Loving others is not some abstract exercise of theory. For Luther and others, serving those closest to us—our family and our literal neighbor—was the greatest physical manifestation of our love of God. The exciting thing is that in some spiritual way, by loving others we are expressing God's love in a tangible way in another person's life.

Theologian Gary Badcock echoes this thought, saying, "The question of vocation, 'What will I do with my life?' is one that can be answered for the Christian only in terms of love, for love is the way of Christ himself, and the way of the God who sent him into the world."[6] Somehow, and sadly, in much of Western Christianity, we seem to have forgotten this. God has not called us to live on some island of self-existence. Self-sufficiency is just an illusion of pride. Each person belongs to each other, like pieces of a finely crafted puzzle. Your God-given callings are not to be hoarded and kept only for your own benefit. They are to be used in love for the benefit of others.

As I have already said, do not confuse your functional callings with your career choice alone. Scripture does not equate following one's callings with earning a paycheck. Moreover, completely identifying yourself with your career is dangerous. In fact, the most important things people do in life are usually the things that they are not paid to do. Every rightful human task is some aspect of God's own work: making, designing, doing chores, beautifying, organizing, helping, bringing dignity, and leading. Our work then is to reflect God's work. As the apostle Paul proclaims, "Work willingly at whatever you do, as though you were working for the Lord rather than for people" (Col. 3:23, NLT).

You may be among those who will have the wonderful opportunity to receive a paycheck as you live out your functional callings in the body of Christ. But the vast majority of people find their functional callings in the body of Christ and in the everyday world without a paycheck from a church. The city employee, the pastor, the construction worker, the missionary, the farmer, the professor, the artist, the schoolteacher, the salesperson, the stay-at-home mom, the utility worker, and the retired person all serve functions in the body of Christ and in the greater world.

Educator William Placher, in his recent compilation *Callings: Twenty Centuries of Christian Wisdom on Vocation*, reflects, "Christianity has preserved the fundamental idea that our lives count for something because God has a direction in mind for them. . . . If the God who made us has figured out something we are supposed to do, . . . then . . . my story has meaning as part of a larger story, ultimately shaped by God."[7]

Uncovering Your Functional Callings

Recognizing God's sovereignty allows your life to reflect God's intentions. The theology of God's sovereignty teaches that God's plan has no accidents or surprises (Ps. 139:13-16; Job 10:8-12). If you believe in a sovereign God, then you also believe that a fit exists between who you are and what God desires you to do. Your heritage, geography, personality, learning style, giftings, life experiences, opportunities, values, and passions all come ultimately from the hand of God. Fate and chance do not rule your life. Even your limitations and your concerns are under God's watchful eye.

In their book *The Power of Uniqueness*, Arthur Miller and William Hendricks, consultants in human development, tell readers, "you are the customized expression of a loving God. . . . You have been endowed with a unique mix of competencies and the desire and drive to use them in pursuit of an outcome of unrivaled personal importance. Your life has meaning built into it."[8]

In discovering your functional callings, finding your unique mix is important. In the simplest terms, callings are the places in life where God has brought you, where God's purpose and your uniqueness come together in love for God and love for others. To be true to yourself is to be true to how God has made you. Living your true identity rather than living out a false image is vital to your survival in ministry—and to your survival in life.

In *Let Your Life Speak*, educational activist and author Parker Palmer warns, "The deepest vocational question is . . . 'Who am I? What is my nature? . . .' If you seek vocation without understanding the material you are working with, what you build with your life will be ungainly and may well put lives in peril, your own and some of those around you."[9]

Living a life out of a false image may be the truest definition of a hypocrite. Our word *hypocrisy* comes from the Greek *hypokrisis*, which means the act of playing a part on the stage.[10] In lacking an understanding of who God made you to be, you instead live the life of an actor playing a part. God does not ask you to wear a mask on the stage of life. To be true to who you are is to be true to how God has made you.

God-Given Giftings

I am a nonmechanical person who married into a family of mechanical people. Now, I am not saying I am all thumbs, but I find many fix-it projects, beyond basic repairs, are out of my league. So, the mechanical and technical skills of my wife's extended family amaze me. I am always hearing stories about what my father-in-law or my brothers-in-law are constructing, building, welding, creating, and so on. While I am only able to look with bewilderment at the engine of my car when I raise the hood, my father-in-law or one of my brothers-in-law can tell you all the intricate details of engine dynamics. While I stand in horror watching water cascading in areas of my house that are supposed to be dry, another brother-in-law is able to rescue me with his plumbing knowledge. Truly amazing.

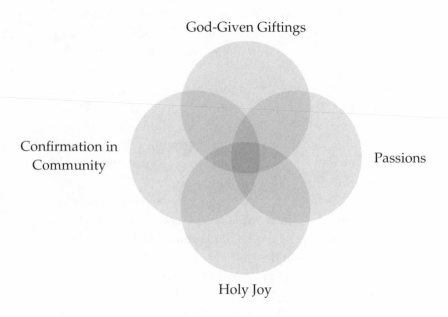

Figure 2.2. Uncovering Your Functional Callings

God did not make you skilled in all areas and God did not make you like anyone else. I know that a world full of George Hillmans would not be a pleasant place to be. Instead, God, with infinite wisdom, made each of us with certain strengths and made other people with other strengths. Knowing what you do well is valuable knowledge. Your God-given strengths, or what I call "giftings," are clear markers of how God made you.

All believers in Jesus Christ are blessed by God with certain abilities and strengths to serve others in love. These actions of love toward others are nothing short of Christ himself ministering to others through us, in both the miraculous and the mundane. The important thing is not the talent or the action, but ultimately the edification of others in love empowered by the Holy Spirit (Eph. 4:11-16).

To understand your callings, you need to assess your giftings. I intentionally use the word *giftings* because even the strengths that you think you have *developed* yourself are a gift from God in the first place. Your divine design reveals aspects of God's functional callings for your life. Ministering out of who you are is key to Spirit-empowered effectiveness and joy in your life and ministry.

In discovering one's giftings, former Gallup Organization researchers Marcus Buckingham and Donald Clifton ask the person to "isolate the tense" he or she is thinking of when performing a particular task. Are you thinking, "When will this be over?" or are you thinking, "When can I do this again?" If you are asking the former, then you are probably operating outside of your giftings. If you are asking the latter, it is a good sign that you are operating in your giftings.[11]

Buckingham and Clifton expand this idea by asking the following questions in helping to identify personal strengths:

1. When performing a task, what are your spontaneous top-of-mind reactions to the situations you encounter, which reveal the location of strong mental connections?
2. What have been your yearnings since childhood, the yearnings that keep calling you, demanding to be heard?
3. When you are faced with learning a new task, are there some skills that you are able to learn more rapidly than others?
4. When the task is over, do you feel a sense of satisfaction?[12]

Taking one of the many inventories available on the market can help you better understand your unique gifts. One of the best

I have found is *The Power of Uniqueness* by Arthur Miller and William Hendricks.[13] Their material helps you identify motivated abilities, motivating subject matter, motivating circumstances (work conditions and settings), operating relationships, and emotional payoff. Another great tool for gifts discovery is the book *Discovering Your Natural Talents* by John Bradley and Jay Carty.[14] Their material helps you discover how you communicate, relate to others, function, and lead. In addition, ask your school's internship coordinator or your pastor for suggested resources that he or she would recommend. You might use one of these resources in conjunction with reading this book.

In addition to these and other widely available inventories, ask the people who know you best what giftings they see in your life. As I discuss below, your community of relationships is vital to this process, offering you both perspective and balance.

While some people have served using skills that were not their inherent giftings for that particular ministry task, those examples are very rare. God's normal mode of operation is to equip those God has commissioned for service. Moreover, when the alignment of giftedness and environment occurs, God-honoring and God-empowered ministry takes place. When this ministry calibration has occurred in your life, you have known it and the people receiving your grace gifts have known it too. However, the reverse is also true. When you have tried to force yourself into a role that was never meant for you, you have felt the frustration and—guess what?—the people receiving your ill-fitting efforts have known it too.

Passions

In college I was the king of changing majors. When I started, I wanted to be a medical doctor. That career choice sounded like a noble pursuit. I had good grades in high school and I liked science, so I thought it was a fit. However, during my second semester in college, I took my first biology lab class and my perspective changed.

Our big project in the biology lab for the semester was dissecting a fetal pig. Our lab teaching assistant gave us students worksheets on which we noted the various discoveries we were making by filling in the blanks: how big is the heart, where is the liver, and so on. Before long I noticed that I was finishing my worksheets well before everyone else. I just wanted to finish my worksheet on the pig and move on. I noticed that other students, on the other hand, were being meticulous in their pig examination.

After working on our pigs for a few weeks, our teaching assistant announced that we could take our pigs home to study before the final exam. I thought to myself, "Excuse me. Who is going to take their pig home?" As it turned out, I was the only person who did not take his pig home that day.

The other members of that lab had a passion for science. Now, do not get me wrong. I enjoyed class. I loved learning the facts about this animal or that. And it was not a question of skill, because I could do the work. However, I did not have the same passion as these other students. I could do the work, but it was a chore for me. These other students would make wonderful surgeons, with painstaking accuracy in their work. Unfortunately, I would have probably ended up being the doctor with all of the liability cases because of my shoddy work. I changed my major the week after that pig exam.

Along with your giftings and closely aligned with them, God has developed within you certain passions. Some theologians have called this passion "internal oughtness" or "compulsion." The Holy Spirit not only equips us for loving service but also constrains us in certain directions in both the church and the world.[15] Passion is that thing you cannot not do. God has shaped you to have certain subjects, objects, or concerns that motivate you. You become more energized and work better in an area you are passionate about.

Discovering the root meaning of the word *passion* is a humbling thing. In addition to the common understanding of *passion* as an emotional stirring, the word also means "suffering," as in Acts 1:3, where Luke talks about the sufferings of Jesus on the cross. So at its heart, passion means suffering. To expand this line of thought, passions are those things you are willing to suffer for in their pursuit. According to Parker Palmer, the passion part of your callings states in your life, "This is something I cannot not do, for reasons I am unable to explain to anyone else and do not fully understand myself but that are nonetheless compelling."[16]

Can passions be used in a bad way? Of course. Each of us has the potential for acting in self-serving ways. Pursuit of passions for self-fulfillment is foreign to the testimony of both Scripture and two thousand years of church history. For example, the apostle Paul writes that we are still "of flesh" in this world (Rom. 7:13-25; Eph. 2:3; Gal. 5:16). In several letters he speaks of passion in a negative light (Rom. 1:26; Col. 3:5; 1 Thess. 4:5). Even with the most noble of passions, we can easily become self-serving. The point is to love God completely, love others compassionately, and love ourselves correctly.

However, when God's word is the center of your life, the Holy Spirit empowers your life and God aligns your passions to God's desires. As you walk close to God in your daily life, God is able to shape both your character and your passions.[17] As King David noted, "Delight yourself in the LORD, and he will give you the desires of your heart" (Ps. 37:4).

You can begin to discover your passions by asking the following questions:

1. What topics or activities excite you?
2. What topics or activities keep you up at night?

3. What topics or activities cause you to jump out of bed in the morning?
4. What are the themes of the greatest accomplishments in your life?
5. What activities or discussions cause you to lose track of time because you are so focused?
6. Where do you feel like you are making a difference?[18]

You do not have to spend much time with other people to discover that each of us has different passions. While one person might be passionate about missions in Africa, another person is passionate about working with junior high students. Is either of these passions better than the other? Of course not. The beauty of God's creation is that each of us has different passions so that the complete mosaic of ministry takes place. God has so shaped us that our gifts, when used for God's purposes, complement one another.[19]

In my eclectic ministry employment, I served for a brief time as a youth minister. The congregation I was serving at the time had lost its youth minister and I filled in for the summer, in addition to keeping my other responsibilities at the church. While I cannot begin to tell you how important youth ministry is and how great the need is, I made a terrible youth minister. I had the abilities and experience to be a youth minister, but I did not have the passion for that ministry. Instead of looking forward to a summer full of student camps and mission trips, I came to dread the summer activities. I know that the parents and the kids were thankful that fall when we were able to hire a new youth minister.

Now that my daughter is becoming involved in the youth ministry at our church, I am so thankful for the men and women who serve in that ministry. Why? Because these people are passionate about my daughter's spiritual, emotional, and interpersonal development. These leaders with the right strengths and passions minister to our family.

As I am writing this chapter, I am looking forward to dinner tonight with our church's student ministry pastor and his family. This is a man who even gets excited about working with junior high boys. Wow! That astounds me still. I thank God for people with both the abilities and the passions for life's varied ministries.

Holy Joy

Out of your God-given giftings and passions, joy becomes a natural byproduct. Some of life's deepest satisfactions come when people are freely expressing their giftings and passions in loving service to others. Please understand—joy is not the goal. But joy is one fruit of the Spirit, an outgrowth of the Spirit-led life (Rom. 5:1-5; Gal. 5:22-23; Col. 3:12-17).

Reflecting on things that bring you joy in life is not self-serving, if you maintain a proper perspective. Personal joy, significance, meaning, and fulfillment focused on a God-given purpose are hallmarks of a believer's life.[20] The author of Ecclesiastes says it this way: "There is nothing better for a person than that he should eat and drink and find enjoyment in his toil. This also, I saw, is from the hand of God, for apart from him who can eat or who can have enjoyment? For to the one who pleases him God has given wisdom and knowledge and joy, but to the sinner he has given the business of gathering and collecting, only to give to one who pleases God. This also is vanity and a striving after wind" (2:24-26).

Jesus speaks directly on the joy that comes as a result of faithfulness. In his parable on faithfulness and its results in Matthew 25:14-30, Jesus talks about three f's of serving: faithfulness, fruitfulness, and fulfillment. In the parable, Jesus tells of three servants who receive varying amounts of money from their master for safekeeping during their master's travels. While the teaching in this parable is primarily eschatological in nature, concerning future judgment, the teaching also emphasizes the faithfulness of the servants, the fruitfulness of the servants' care of the master's estate, and the resulting joy from faithful stewardship.

To the two servants who were faithful and fruitful with what the master entrusted, the master gladly proclaimed, "Well done, good and faithful servant. You have been faithful over a little; I will set you over much. Enter into the joy of your master" (Matt. 25:21, 23). Notice that the reward for the faithful and fruitful servants was not a bonus in their paycheck. A servant working for a master has no need for money in the first place. The reward to the faithful and fruitful servants was the privilege to enter into and share the master's joy. This was not self-made joy. The joy was a gift from the master.

The paradox of joy in serving is that joy and suffering coexist in the life of the believer. Let no one fool you otherwise—being a Christian and being faithful in loving God and loving others is tough. Just travel back in time and talk with the prophets Jeremiah or Hosea or Jonah. While physical persecution is not currently a widespread reality in Western Christianity, that is not the case with our brothers and sisters in Christ in other parts of the world and throughout history. The apostle Paul cautions that even with heavenly joy set before us, suffering and persecution are real as well (Rom. 8:18; 2 Tim. 3:12).

We feel God's pleasure and experience joy when we live "obediently in the center of a call," as pastor and author Gordon MacDonald says. People have died for obeying the call of God. Others have been called to extremely challenging and discouraging ministries where survival was a daily struggle. Still others have lived out their calling in obscurity, feeling that their efforts have made little difference. But even in these circumstances, one can feel the pleasure of God.[21]

Not everything in ministry or in life is always emotionally joyful or exciting. But much of the joy in ministry and in life comes from understanding that even the simplest acts of love you perform for others can carry with them sacred meaning, whether you ever see tangible results or not. Faith makes all tasks, no matter how trivial or distasteful, equally holy.[22] Believing this, Martin Luther directed young fathers in the mundane task of changing their baby's diaper to imagine that during this act of service they are holding the infant Jesus. If joy does result from fulfilling your callings, consider the blessing of that and be thankful.[23]

The reality is that you cannot continue in effective service without experiencing some joy. The opposite of joy in service is burnout. Instead of thinking of burnout as occurring from attempting too much, in reality burnout occurs when you are trying to give in areas where you do not possess either the giftings or the passions. More than anything, burnout is a state of emptiness where you have nothing to give at all.[24]

Confirmation in Community

One final element to consider as you uncover your functional callings is the role of the community of faith. Community is essential in spiritual discernment of functional callings, especially as you consider how to serve within the local church. The call to faith occurs in community. A transformed life is lived out in community. The purpose of your functional callings is loving service of others. Sober judgment of your functional callings can only take place in community. And trust me, community keeps you humble.

In *Listening to God in Times of Choice: The Art of Discerning God's Will*, Gordon T. Smith, missiologist and educator, reminds us, "Every significant choice we make reflects the fact that we are profoundly interconnected with the lives of others. Our decisions inevitably affect others but are affected by the choices that others make. It is only appropriate that we are accountable to others in our choices."[25]

Consistent with Scripture and with two thousand years of church history, the community of faith typically affirms functional callings through the local church. This is often referred to as "corporate calling." Theologians discuss the idea of a person receiving both a personal, inward calling and a corporate, outward calling. I strongly believe that when God calls a person into a functional ministry, the body of Christ confirms that calling. God's normal mode of operation (again, exceptions exist but they are rare) is, I believe, the public confirmation of one's functional callings as the community of faith sees the person function and as the Holy Spirit directs the actions of the community of faith.

In discussing this idea of corporate calling, former field educator at Midwestern Baptist Theological Seminary Ray Kesner writes, "Until a body of believers calls you to a specific ministry function, you cannot say with certainty that God has called you to some particular ministry role."[26]

Calling in a corporate setting is a natural extension of the scriptural mandate for godly counsel. Seeking wise counsel is a strong biblical theme, especially in Proverbs. Here is a brief sampling:

- "Let the wise hear and increase in learning, and the one who understands obtain guidance" (Prov. 1:5).
- "The way of a fool is right in his own eyes, but a wise man listens to advice" (Prov. 12:15).
- "Listen to advice and accept instruction, that you may gain wisdom in the future" (Prov. 19:20).

Because of the human ability for self-deception, it is essential for you to seek an outside perspective from others. You might think you are the next great preacher or the next cutting-edge biblical scholar, but do the other people around you see the same thing in you? Do they see the giftings and passions that you perceive as yours? Do your teachers and classmates see the same competence that you see in your life? If you are to be honest with God, you need to be open to the honest assessment of those who know you well.

Testing Your Functional Callings

Many of you reading this chapter are in college or seminary and, therefore, in the process of confirming or nullifying different aspects of your vocational understanding. Testing your functional callings is what you are supposed to do during this time in your life. A great internship can help confirm or nullify different aspects of vocational understanding. As I constantly tell students who come into my office, it is much better to discover now what God is calling you to do than to spend thousands of dollars in tuition, move your family to the middle of nowhere, and discover that you hate what you have been trained to do.

For example, for a ministry student to have grand and glorious visions of being a missionary to another country or region of the world is one thing. Living on the mission field for a semester and discovering the reality of missions work is quite another, once the tough nature of the task becomes reality. The student who is truly called to the mission field will find the experience challenging but confirming and fulfilling. The student who is not called to the mission field will only feel frustrated.

David Ward, my predecessor at Dallas Theological Seminary, has described internships as serving students in at least three ways—as confirmation, as clarification, or as catalyst.[27]

Confirmation of Callings

If you are a student with clear vocational vision, an internship will provide confirmation to your known call and vocational direction. Your internship experience will verify what you already know. A veteran missionary, for example, returning to seminary to retool from a church-planting focus to a Bible-college teaching and administration focus could complete an internship in a formal classroom teaching setting. This student would discover quickly if he or she enjoys developing syllabi and lesson plans.

Clarification of Callings

For other students, an internship will assist you in clarifying your call and vocational direction without a long-term commitment. At most schools, this is probably the experience of the vast majority of the student population. In these cases, an internship serves as a trial run to see if a fit is noticeable. For instance, a counseling student completing an internship with a women's shelter will discover quickly if she enjoys the demands of seeing clients and facilitating support groups on a daily basis. If because of her internship this student decides that she does not enjoy intensive counseling, she is better off discovering this now than graduating with a counseling degree and taking a job she will find frustrating and dread.

Catalyst for Call Discovery

Finally, for some students, an internship will serve as a catalyst for discerning your call and the need for vocational development. You may have arrived on campus with no idea of vocational direction. The internship process and the wise words of an internship site supervisor might be just what you need to get pointed in the right direction.

The Dance of Discernment

Sometimes I think in their search for direction people long for the guidance the Israelites had in the days of the exodus. During their desert travels, "the LORD went before them by day in a pillar of cloud to lead them along the way, and by night in a pillar of fire to give them light, that they might travel by day and by night. The pillar of cloud by day and the pillar of fire by night did not depart from before the people" (Ex. 13:21-22).

In certain moments of life and at certain crossroads, you might think how much easier life would be if you could simply follow the trail of cloud and fire. If only every major decision of life could be accompanied by a supernatural trail marker like those pillars, how great life would be.

Does God speak to people today? Absolutely! For you, God's leadings are no less spiritual but may be less dramatic. However, you have three things the children of Israel did not. First, you have God's word in written form to offer guidance in your life. Second, you have the indwelling Holy Spirit. While only a select few of the Old Testament saints had the temporary dwelling of the Holy Spirit in their life (1 Sam. 16:14; Ps. 51:11), all believers in Jesus Christ have the Holy Spirit as a permanent counselor, an advocate, and a helper (John 14:15-30; Rom. 5:5; Rom. 8:9; 1 Cor. 2:12; 1 Cor. 3:16; 2 Cor. 5:5). And finally you have the community of faith.

God's Dance Partner

Instead of living in the age of the dramatic, we believers in Jesus Christ live in the age of the dance. What do I mean? Gordon T. Smith in *Listening to God in Times of Choice* paints this beautiful word picture: "Discernment, indeed the whole Christian experience . . . is like a dance with God. God in his love and holiness invites us into a dialogue, a conversation, a relationship that includes not only submission but also the engagement of our will and our freedom with God."[28]

While we might long for God's presence in the pillar of cloud and fire, dancing with a cloud or a flame is not possible.

Instead of distance, God desires intimacy with his children. God is known not by objective detachment but in loving transformational devotion.[29] As he prepares the next generation of Israelites to enter the promised land at the end of their desert wanderings, Moses reminds the people, "You have seen how the LORD your God carried you, as a man carries his son, all the way that you went until you came to this place" (Deut. 1:31).

One Christmas, my daughter received *Barbie in The Nutcracker* on DVD as a gift from my wife and me. Before our purchase of this DVD, I probably could not have told you a single thing about "The Nutcracker" story and ballet (either the Barbie variety or otherwise). But as any good dad would do, I watched the movie with my daughter too many times to count. After a while, I could even whistle the tunes and quote most of the lines. However, my daughter wanted to do more than watch *Barbie in The Nutcracker*. She wanted to experience *Barbie in The Nutcracker*. Therefore, at the story's big climax she would get up and dance the role of Barbie in the grand finale. And you cannot have a dancing Barbie without a dancing Ken. Because I am the only male in the house, you can guess who got the part of dancing Ken.

As I write this, I am smiling because those days of being dancing Ken with my daughter are some of my most special memories. My daughter has since moved on past Barbies, but now and then I still steal a dance with my daughter. She dances with zeal to the music, but she would only dance when her dance partner danced with her.

God desires to dance with you. As I have said throughout this chapter, your primary calling to God is paramount. God desires to draw you close in a relationship, to mold you into the likeness of his Son. God does not simply want to give you answers to your questions. God wants to dance with you. No quicksteps exist in the dance of discernment; it is a slow dance. Discernment is the spiritual exercise of drawing near the heartbeat of God so that God can lead you in the dance of life.

Pastor Charles Swindoll, in his book *The Mystery of God's Will*, confesses, "Our human tendency is to focus solely on our calling—on where we should go, how we should get there, and what exactly we should do about it. God's concern is the process . . . to mature us and ready us, making us more like His Son. In other words, all of us—including you—are works in process."[30]

Slowing Down to Dance

Some people think a call from God can only come through some type of cataclysmic emotional experience. In reality, most people recognize aspects of God's leadings as gradual in nature as they experience life. In fact, when you depend on the emotionally dramatic, you are many times less likely to stick with the commitments driven by emotional impulses alone.

The key to learning the dance steps of discernment is prayer along with sound biblical study. You discern the leadings of God in the dancing relationship. You must remain in close communication with God to have any chance of discerning well. Instead of focusing your prayers on God revealing his will, focus on God creating godly character and wisdom in you. When your actions, thoughts, and desires reflect God's priorities, then you are in a better place to discern well.

The problem with discernment is that many of us are so busy doing our own thing, moving too fast to dance the slow dance of discernment with God. You can only hear the heartbeat of God in your life when you slow down, quiet yourself, and invite God to dance with you. To slow down and listen takes a concerted and countercultural effort. The lights and sounds of society distract us if we are not careful. My digital video recorder always has new television programs for me to watch. My cell phone always has messages that need immediate answers. My local coffee shop has Internet Wi-Fi so I am always connected to my e-mail at work. My MP3 player always has music and podcasts for me to listen to. There are always meetings for me to attend. With all of this and much more vying for my attention, I must be intentional about disconnecting and taking time to hear what God is saying.

Are You Ready to Dance?

What God ultimately wants is you and to spend time with you. The mystery that the infinite God of the universe desires a relationship with lowly humanity is beyond my comprehension, but I am so thankful that God desires the relationship. As psychologist David Benner puts it, "What God wants is simply our presence, even if it feels like a waste of potentially productive time. That is what friends do together—they waste time with each other. Simply being together is enough without expecting to 'get something' from the interaction. It should be no different with God."[31]

So, if you have noticed, we have come full circle. The underpinning to your life is your call to a love relationship with God through salvation in Jesus Christ and to develop that love relationship through the sanctifying power of the Holy Spirit. Out of this primary call come the functional callings to love others in your sphere of influence. You discover your functional callings as you continue to learn who you are through dancing in a love relationship with God.

So put on your dancing shoes and enjoy the dance.

Questions for Reflection

1. How has your understanding of the call of God changed over the years?

2. What direction did you feel called to when you first
   came to school? What direction do you feel called to
   now?
3. Think about your God-given giftings? What are they?
4. What passions have you identified? What ministry areas
   might they relate to?
5. What tasks give you the greatest sense of joy? How
   might they be part of your ministry?
6. How have other people affirmed you in your sense of
   calling? What giftings do they observe in you?
7. Do you find dancing with God for discernment exciting
   or frustrating? Why?

CHAPTER 3

What Are the Ingredients for a Healthy Internship?

I HAVE A CONFESSION TO MAKE. I LOVE WATCHING THE Food Network on television at night. Do not ask me why, because I am not sure. I am not a great chef, nor do I pretend to be. Nevertheless, I love watching shows that tell me how my favorite foods are made.

Last week, for example, my family watched a show on how to make pizza dough. Will I ever actually take the time to make my own pizza dough from scratch? Probably not, but I was fascinated by the show's host explaining the science behind pizza dough and the specific ingredients needed for perfect dough. Besides becoming hungry, I learned once again the reasons why certain ingredients are imperative.

Two factors and foci evident in all the cooking shows I watch are the right ingredients and the right preparation. Ingredients do make a difference. Frozen pizza is just not the same as pizza made from scratch with fresh ingredients. Like any great recipe, the quality of any product at the end depends on the quality of the ingredients at the beginning.

An internship is no different. The ingredients and the preparation make all of the difference. In my experience, great internships start with the following essential ingredients:

1. A proactive intern
2. A caring mentor
3. A beneficial internship site

Let me elaborate on each of these.

Being a Proactive Intern

I cannot emphasize enough the significance of your own initiative. *This is your internship.* This is not the school's internship. This is not the denomination's internship. This is not the church's or organization's internship. This is not the mentor's or supervisor's internship. *This is your internship.* You as the student need to pursue an active role in all aspects of the internship. You need to be the driving force behind the learning process—the motivational source—and own the mentoring relationship.

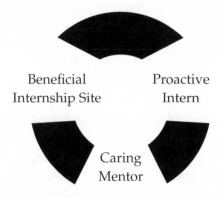

Beneficial
Internship Site

Proactive
Intern

Caring
Mentor

Figure 3.1 Ingredients of a Healthy Internship

Learner-Centered Education

For most students, not only ministry students, superimposed structures have dictated their entire educational career. As a result, many students have been passive participants in their educational development. The educational system tells them what classes to take, what pages to study for the test, how long their book report needs to be, and so on. This powerlessness of the learner causes the student to not pursue personal goals but instead to try to jump through the hoops of education, only caring about getting a good grade or making the teacher happy. Sadly, many ministry students approach their internship in the same passive way.

My experience working with hundreds of ministry students shows that the intern who takes the initiative is much more likely to have a fulfilling internship than the more passive intern is. You get out of the internship what you put into the internship. Proactive interns do not procrastinate. Taking the initiative will help you be assertive in assessing your developmental needs and goals even before the internship begins. By being proactive, you will also be able to find an internship site that meets these discovered needs and goals. Finally, by taking the initiative, you will be able to assimilate more quickly into the organization where you are serving.[1]

Instead of the school or internship mentor taking you by the hand, you need to take ownership of the learning alliance created between you, the school, and your mentor. The mentor's job or the school's job is not to give you all the answers. Rather, their job is to ask the right questions to help you discover the answers. When you lead the relationship, you will generally learn more quickly and retain more. When you discover the answers rather than having the answers given to you, you are also more likely to follow through on the needed action points because you came up with the steps first.

When my wife and I first became parents, we did not lack for parental advice and nuggets of truth from just about everyone. When you are a new parent, everybody you meet has a word of wisdom about raising kids or a hidden parenting fact to tell you. Do you know what my wife and I did with most of that advice? You guessed it—we ignored it. At the time, we thought that we had the entire parenting thing figured out. We did not feel the need to take any advice.

Thank goodness, our arrogance was whittled away as we learned on our own that we were not yet qualified to be the super parents we thought we were. Once we discovered we did not know all the techniques to get our daughter to sleep at night, we were much more open to listening to advice from others. Forced advice on an unreceptive person is rarely heard. However, once a need is met by well-timed advice, change happens.

Our experience as new parents is consistent with modern adult-education theory. Adults learn best when they have ownership of, authority for, and self-direction in their education, including diagnosing, planning, implementing, and evaluating, and when they have a readiness and eagerness to learn based on their perceived needs.[2] If you are motivated, ready to learn, teachable, and willing to take ownership, then the internship experience will more likely be both enjoyable and educational. You are not pursuing an internship only to get a good grade or to make the school happy. You are pursuing an internship to prepare yourself for lifelong ministry. If you are proactive, then your mentor will be better able to help you articulate your passions and to help you clarify your purpose and goals.

The "Dream" Intern

Mentors and teachers want to see a student who is self-motivated and who takes responsibility for his or her own growth and development. The simple fact is that the more eager you are to learn, the more eager the mentor is to teach. As my colleague Howard Hendricks at Dallas Theological Seminary describes,

> I prefer to invest [my time and energy] in people who essentially burn on their own once the match has ignited their kindling. . . . If you're not eager to learn, there are very few people who are willing to . . . invest the energy that it takes to light a fire under your curiosity and imagination. . . . Those who have something to teach you will invariably find a way to let you drink from their wealth of knowledge if you convince them that you are genuinely interested. . . . As a mentor, the last thing I have time to do is to set someone's agenda. . . . I'm more than happy to hold his feet to the fire for the agenda he sets.[3]

You and your mentor are active collaborators in the internship. Nevertheless, you ultimately need to be the one setting the agenda. The school or your mentor can help influence your developmental agenda, but they should not set it. Your mentor's job is not to chase you down. Your mentor's job is to make sure that the agenda does not get lost during the internship.[4]

Working alongside a Caring Mentor

We have already established the central role you as the intern play in your own development, at the same time recognizing that your development does not happen in isolation. The second ingredient in the internship recipe is a caring mentor. The direction of a mentor is priceless to a promising leader.[5] As in athletics where growth and change do not happen without a relationship with a coach or trainer, so too in preparation for ministry a person needs someone who is able to provide resources, assessment, motivation, and accountability. Spiritual formation and personal growth happen best in relationships. Regina Coll in *Supervision of Ministry Students* says that mentoring is an interpersonal partnership where the mentor "takes on the responsibility of cooperating with the student in the pursuit of ministerial skills, in the development of a ministerial identity, and in bringing book knowledge into dialogue with the life of the community."[6]

Educators Keith Anderson and Randy Reese, in their book *Spiritual Mentoring*, offer the following reminder: "Spiritual formation, education of the heart, in other words, requires something more than traditional Western forms of instruction. It requires a mentorship of the heart, a relationship with a teacher of life who is able to convey what was learned from the teacher's own faithful mentor, a way of life that is formed, not merely instructions that are given. . . . We come to the realization that we need help, that we are not meant to make this journey solo. We learn to listen to the voices of mentors, not as absolute experts with the final authoritative word but more as the shrewd and discerning expressions of those who have traveled this way before."[7]

Qualities of a Mentoring Relationship

Where you serve as an intern and selecting an appropriate site are certainly important to your internship experience; however, your ministry mentor at the internship site is more important than the actual location. A fantastic internship site with a poor mentor is worse than an adequate internship site with a great mentor. In directing the internship program at my school, the number one complaint of students who have had a poor internship experience is the lack of a relationship with their mentor. One-on-one time with a caring mentor is the key to the internship's success or failure.

A word of clarification: the individual student at our school selects his or her own internship site and mentor based on his or her degree track—pastoral leadership, cross-cultural ministries, educational leadership, women's ministry, and so forth. We give our students the freedom to pitch their internship ideas to our department for approval. But I know that other schools have very different methods of matching students with mentors and internship sites. At some schools, the student will have a limited number of approved internship sites and mentors to choose from. And at other schools, the school or the denomination will actually place the student in an internship site and with a mentor, with the student having limited input into the process. But no matter the system, the same mentoring qualities are vital for success.

So, are you supposed to look for Superman or Wonder Woman in a mentor? Of course not. No mentor possesses every ideal quality and characteristic. Mentors are as unique as the individual relationship. A mentor does not have to be perfect or an expert to have an impact on your life, but some basic qualities do exist. A caring mentor exhibits the following:

1. Actively teaches and serves as a resource
2. Attentively listens
3. Creates an environment of trust
4. Courageously loves

A CARING MENTOR ACTIVELY TEACHES AND SERVES AS A RESOURCE

Think of your internship as you would any other class. Just as you would sit under the tutelage of a Greek or church history professor, you need to see your mentor as a teacher as well. However, instead of being in the formal classroom on campus, you are now in class in the field. The purpose of the internship is not for the church, the denomination, or the ministry organization

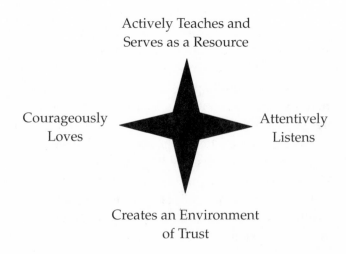

Actively Teaches and
Serves as a Resource

Courageously
Loves

Attentively
Listens

Creates an Environment
of Trust

Figure 3.2. Qualities of a Caring Mentor

to get cheap summer help for their projects. Its purpose is to help you reach your God-given potential, and your mentor's role is to help create an environment for your learning and growth. Find a mentor who is focused on your growth, not on using you as a gofer.

Be on the lookout for growth opportunities at the internship site and beyond it. Some learning will come naturally from the given job description for the internship, but some opportunities for growth will need to be created as the two of you serve together. This might be especially true in a smaller church or organizational setting. Explore with your mentor potential learning opportunities that will expose you to new experiences as well as reinforce new learning. Also work with your mentor to identify opportunities that might accelerate learning.[8]

Besides being a teacher, a mentor acts as a resource. With the unbelievable amount of ministry information available, being aware of the vast resources for ministry is impossible for you as a student. A mentor brings his or her professional experience and personal network to an internship that connect you to developmental resources and ideas.

What kinds of resources? Consider asking your mentor all of the following questions:

- What professional organizations does your mentor recommend joining?
- What publishing organizations focus on your particular ministry area?
- What books, magazines, and journals does your mentor recommend reading?
- What Web sites have relevant information devoted to your particular ministry area?
- Who are the local, national, and international leaders you need to meet?
- How do you get to know these leaders?
- What conferences, retreat centers, and training opportunities do you need to attend?
- What tricks of the trade do you need to learn that you did not learn at school?

So, what does a mentor look like who takes the role of an active teacher and resource person seriously? Let me illustrate. Suppose you are at school preparing to be a music minister. For your summer internship, you are working with a local music minister at a church. Your job description might include assisting in the summer worship services, supporting the church's pastoral staff in directing the worship team or the choir, coordinating the church's children's summer music camp, and organizing the church's Fourth of July musical community outreach. With such a busy summer, you will have plenty of learning opportunities built into the process simply by the nature of fulfilling the job description. Among them will be learning about public worship leadership, leadership of teams, interpersonal skills, budgeting, and vision casting.

While much learning will take place automatically during this busy summer, a mentor can help you in several ways. You might already possess good worship leadership skills, and a mentor would be able to help you refine those skills throughout the summer. When you are asked to do something that you have never done before, a mentor can direct you to appropriate resources, help you brainstorm possibilities, or be a sounding board for your ideas. When you observe the music minister handle a complicated situation with relative ease and you wonder how he or she did that, your mentor can take you through the mental steps he or she went through to arrive at the solution. While assisting in your first funeral, your mentor helps you process your theological reflections. Through your mentor, you are introduced to other local music ministers from a wide variety of denominations and worship traditions. Your mentor might take you to a national worship conference and introduce you to a worshiping network or to publishing resources you were unaware of. That is how a mentor can turn a good summer of learning into a great summer of learning.

Remember that sometimes the ministry superstars are not the best teachers of how they do what they do. These leaders are excellent at what they do (preaching, teaching, managing), but they may not be able to articulate their process to you. You need to find a mentor who can clearly explain why and how they do what they do. You want to learn certain information from your mentor. A mentor is one who is established in the foundations of ministry and can impart both the content skills and the people skills of ministry in a clear way.

A CARING MENTOR ATTENTIVELY LISTENS

Hand in hand with the role of teacher, a mentor needs to be an attentive listener. A mentor does not have to have all the answers to every question. The mentor is not there to "lecture, opine, or pontificate."[9] Many times the vital role a mentor can play is as a sounding board or a mirror for you. A mentor asks, listens, affirms, shares, and empathizes with you in a timely manner.

To truly be heard by another person is a powerful experience, but it is a rare experience because most people do not listen at a deep level. Admittedly, all of us are guilty of being distracted, half listening and half thinking, at times during a conversation. Great mentoring "requires masterful listening, attuned and adept, with the ability to maximize the listening interaction. Interaction is the right word, too, because listening is not simply passively hearing. There is action in listening."[10]

Active listening occurs when the hearer intentionally focuses on the speaker to truly understand what is being said. Active listening involves hearing verbal content (word choice and structure), perceiving nonverbal content (posture, tone, eye contact, timing, gestures), discerning the underlying emotions, and recognizing the context of the communication.[11] An active listener can repeat (in his or her own words) what was said by the speaker to the satisfaction of the speaker for the purposes of mutual understanding, not necessarily for agreement. But beyond the spoken words, an active listener also can sense the underlying emotions being communicated (such as anger, confusion, joy). Instead of racing ahead to think of the next response or assuming to know the answers, an active listener allows him- or herself time to process what is being communicated. Poor listening makes good communication almost unattainable.

The crux of much of the mentoring relationship is listening, especially the mentor listening to you. The questions your mentor needs to ask you are:

- Is this intern on the right track with his or her vision? What evidence do I see?

- Is this intern honoring his or her values? What evidence do I see?
- What is this intern experiencing emotionally?
- Where is this intern going with his or her development?

Real listening in mentoring occurs at a deep level. A caring mentor listens for the "meaning behind the story, for the underlying process, for the theme that will deepen the learning." A caring mentor listens for your vision, values, and purpose and for your struggle, trepidation, backtracking, and "fleshy sabotage"—that is, selfish decisions made in the moment.[12] The influence of mentoring increases as you and your mentor get to know each other better and as your mentor begins to be aware of your strengths, passions, and ministry vision.

Your mentor needs to be listening for signs of life, for the choices you are making, and how those choices are affecting your growth. The mentor is also listening for "resistance and turbulence in the process."[13] As he or she listens to you, your mentor makes changes in the internship to fit your developmental needs. Sometimes those changes will be made on the fly as you and your mentor work together throughout your internship. A good listener will be able to pick up the signals that indicate the need for change.

What does attentive listening sound like? Consider the following. Suppose you have a semester-long internship with a mission organization in another country. While you have traveled to other parts of the world a few times before and arrived at school intending to become a missionary, your internship is your first extended period in a cross-cultural environment. You start off the internship with high expectations of how God will use you this semester.

After a few weeks, the exotic excitement of being in a foreign land has subsided and reality begins setting in. First, you feel the frustration of not speaking the language well enough to communicate clearly with the people you are supposed to be working with. You can catch short phrases and smile in return, but that is about all. As a result of the language barrier, you have not participated in as much hands-on ministry as you originally anticipated. And on top of this language issue and the resulting frustration, you are having a difficult time relating to one of the team members. So, on the outside, things may look great, but inside you are slowly getting more and more agitated. When asked, you tell everyone you are just fine and nothing is wrong.

A good mentor, however, would not be satisfied with your one-word answers and would try to listen to the communication behind the words. Watching your body language and unspoken countenance, your mentor might begin to sense that you have been unsettled the last week or so. With some gentle questions from your mentor, you are finally able to share your frustrations and concerns with a caring recipient. Because of the mentor's willingness to listen, this one exchange could change the direction of and the way you experience the remainder of your internship.

A CARING MENTOR CREATES AN ENVIRONMENT OF TRUST
Recall when you learned how to ride a bicycle? What about the first time you jumped off the diving board into the deep end of the pool? How about your first attempt at ice-skating? Was it scary? Absolutely, but you also probably had a parent, an older sibling, or a friend helping you along the way with these and thousands of other first-time accomplishments. The key to your trying these things in the first place was probably preceded with the words, "Don't worry. I have got you if you fall." These words helped create an environment of trust for you to try, and if you failed a few times, you failed safely.

A good mentor can do the same thing in helping create an environment of trust. This is an environment where you can feel safe to try new things, to explore underlying emotional responses, and to ask the questions you have been dying to ask about ministry and life. In many ways, working in a trusting environment is closely related to having a mentor who attentively listens, described above. In this environment of trust, a dumb question doesn't exist and failure is seen as a pathway to long-term growth. Paramount to this environment of trust is that your self-worth and value are not brought into question.[14]

A trusting environment is foundational to much of the work that will take place in the internship and in the functioning of the mentoring relationship. If you do not feel safe, how will you ever try new things? If you do not feel safe, how will you admit your shortcomings? If you do not feel safe, how will you change? A mutually committed relationship characterized by trust and hope is necessary for change and growth to take place.

Going back to the example of you serving a mission field in another country, you would feel comfortable sharing your frustrations about the language barrier and concern about the other teammate only if the mentor had been intentional in creating a trusting environment from the start. If you did not feel safe, you would try to protect your own self-interests and not say anything. The environment of trust and the action of listening go hand-in-hand in great mentoring.

From your experiences at work, at school, at home, and with friends, you may have learned firsthand about unsafe environments. These kinds of environments are where everything you say or do is held against you. These are environments where you are cut down instead of built up. These are environments where you learn very quickly to become self-protective and not to share too much or not to get too close to others. Like a turtle in a shell, you expose just enough to get where you are going in life but no more.

Look for a mentor whom you can trust. A key is to find a mentor who has been trustworthy in the past with others. Remember, though, that the trust between you and your mentor does not happen overnight. Trust is developed in the little things and over time, as both you and your mentor are able to see this trust played out in real situations.

A CARING MENTOR COURAGEOUSLY LOVES

Do you remember the Hans Christian Andersen fairy tale "The Emperor's New Clothes"? The fairy tale is about an emperor who loved his royal clothing. One day he heard about two tailors who could make the finest clothes from the most beautiful cloth in the world. These tailors, who were really swindlers, said that their special cloth had the special characteristic that it was invisible to anyone who was either stupid or not fit for his or her position.

Well, not to appear either dim-witted or unfit to be a ruler, the emperor did not say anything when he tried on his new wardrobe of nothing. Moreover, all of the townspeople were too scared or embarrassed to say anything either. No one wanted to speak the truth, and instead they lavished lies about how beautiful the emperor's new clothing of nothing was. Only in the end did a child point out the obvious truth that the emperor had nothing on.

In the end, did it really do the emperor any good for the people not to speak truth to him about being naked? Of course not. The same is true for you. Constructive feedback is essential for you if you are to ever develop beyond your existing levels of knowledge and skill. While praise is nice to hear and can give you satisfaction, constructive feedback is what helps you know which direction to move for further development.

Having someone speak loving truth to you now is much better than for you to get fired from your first job after graduation for something that everybody knew about you but were too afraid to mention. Or worse, nothing was said because no one wanted to hurt your feelings. This is the lack of courageous love.

One of the marks of a good mentor is a man or woman who loves courageously. Courageous love speaks truth into the life of another. A mentor has the necessary perspective to look into your life and ministry to see where the gaps are and where God is at work. A mentor must be relational, empowering you in a safe but challenging environment and speaking lovingly and courageously into your life to correct imbalances. This requires patience—both yours and the mentor's—knowing that change is difficult and does not occur quickly.

Encouragement is an aspect of courageous love and an essential practice of biblical community. Consider the following verses: "Therefore encourage one another and build one another up, just as you are doing" (1 Thess. 5:11). "And let us consider how to stir up one another to love and good works, not neglecting to meet together, as is the habit of some, but encouraging one another, and all the more as you see the Day drawing near" (Heb. 10:24-25).

Courageous love can be seen in the mentor's initiative, a response to the Holy Spirit's leading in the relationship, to risk personal rejection and address what is holding another person back from experiencing God's unconditional love. Courageous love involves a relational, intimate, and often confrontational service to others that leads them into a closeness with God they may never experience any other way. This kind of love recognizes the flawed foundations of people's character and the supernatural nature of the task. It takes another person's initiative, empowered by the Spirit, to enter the messes in people's lives so that they can experience deliverance from sin and participate in God's purposes for them.

Factors that Can Make or Break a Mentoring Relationship

In addition to your mentor's qualities and abilities, several other factors contribute to creating a mentoring relationship characterized by loving care:

- Consistent mentor meetings
- Clearly defined relational expectations and boundaries
- Attention to and respect for cultural differences

CONSISTENT MENTOR MEETINGS

Every experience for you during the internship has learning potential. With consistent meetings between you and your mentor, the ministry experiences become life changing. Some schools may call this meeting a supervisory conference, reflection meeting, formation meeting, or another name. This meeting with your mentor may also involve other people, such as members of the lay committee or other interns at the same site. While I refer to the mentor meeting that takes place between a mentor and an intern, please understand that these meetings with your mentor and others may serve a similar role. The primary concern is that you have consistent interaction with others at the internship site for supervision and reflection.

This consistent meeting with your mentor, and in some cases others at the site, is the heart of the internship experience and needs to be a sacred priority for both you and your mentor. These meetings are the backbone of the internship because they provide regular opportunities for communication and instruction.

This time with your mentor is sacred; it needs to have a degree of privacy and be free of interruptions.[15] The time set aside for the meeting needs to be long enough to deal both with the issues of your work and your reflection on it. Remember that your mentor helps create an environment where the Holy Spirit can work in your life so that you can focus on your development. That environment is one of safety, courage, confidentiality, trust, and space to breathe, experiment, and dream.

CLEARLY DEFINED EXPECTATIONS AND BOUNDARIES

A word of caution needs to be given concerning emotional entanglement in mentoring relationships. This unfortunate circumstance can potentially occur in any relationship but especially for those in a mixed-gender mentoring relationship, where a male mentor is working with a female student or a female mentor is working with a male student.

Typically, mixed-gender mentoring involves a male mentor working with a female intern. The reality is that many times women students have a hard time finding women mentors.[16] This is due in large part to the increase in number of female seminary students and the expansion of ministry opportunities for these students. Currently, the number of women in vocational leadership roles is not great enough to meet women students' needs for mentors. In the world of church work, women can sometimes feel isolated.

In a mentoring relationship or any helping relationship, such as a pastoral relationship or a counseling relationship, interpersonal dynamics can get deep enough that the caring love experienced in the relationship can be misinterpreted in a sexual way. If the relational intimacy is greater than in other relationships the person has (either from family or friends) and is misread, the relationship can become emotionally and sexually confusing.[17] Therefore, a clear understanding of expectations and boundaries is imperative.

No matter the level of intimacy, the mentoring relationship is still a professional relationship. Here are some things for both you and your mentor to take into account. First, consider body language. Both of you need to avoid any body language that might appear seductive to the other person. This can be the clothing worn, the physical arrangement of the room, the location of the meetings, and the invasion of personal space. Also remember to pay attention to what is said. Both of you need to avoid topics or humor that could be misinterpreted in a sexual manner.[18]

The guiding principle in mixed-gender mentoring is respecting the other person and his or her feelings. If healthy boundaries and expectations are spelled out, I think it is possible for mixed-gender mentoring to work. In fact, it could be quite beneficial for both parties. Due to the fact that many women see relationships as a catalyst for development, recent research has shown that women learners thrive in a mentoring framework, whether the mentor is male or female.[19] Both men and women can grow from mentoring provided by the opposite sex.

That said, I do not place a student into a mixed-gender mentoring relationship if either the student or the mentor is not comfortable with the situation. Because of values, beliefs, heritage, or past experience, such a relationship may be doomed from the start. Some women simply feel more comfortable working with women and some men simply feel more comfortable working with men. In every one of our program's placements, the staff discusses this issue with our students at the beginning of the internship placement process.

Nevertheless, even in the best of circumstances in a mixed-gender mentoring relationship, both the mentor and you must avoid even the perception of inappropriate behavior. Nothing can destroy one's ministry faster than the accusations of a sexually inappropriate relationship, even if there is no truth behind the accusations.

Finally, both you and your mentor must be sensitive to sexual harassment. Sexual harassment might be initiated by the mentor or someone else in the organization. Sexual harassment occurs when:

- Someone insinuates (hints or suggests) that a job or promotion will be made in exchange for sexual favors or insinuates the opposite—a job will be lost or a demotion will occur if sexual favors are not provided.
- An intimidating, hostile, or offensive work environment is created through the presence of offensive (sexual or otherwise) images, language, or behavior.[20]

If either you or your mentor feel that sexual harassment is taking place, dealing with it immediately according to your school's, denomination's, or organization's policies or grievance system is vital. Do not hesitate to talk with the school's internship coordinator.

ATTENTION TO AND RESPECT FOR CULTURAL DIFFERENCES

One of the joys on my campus is the opportunity to interact with future Christian leaders from all over the world. In a single day, I might have students from India, South Korea, China, Brazil, and Russia in my office for appointments. The world is coming to our campuses. Moreover, the world has become smaller through technology, communication, and travel. Therefore, we need to know how to interact with other cultures.

I also enjoy having the opportunity to work with a racially diverse student population. In a single week, I might have an internship site visit with a predominately African American church, an Asian American church, and a Hispanic church. In my classes I will have students representing a racial mix not present in Southern schools a generation or two ago.

The culture of a people affects how they express themselves, and appreciating the rich contributions of different cultures is important for this global community we live in. When confronted with a culture different from our own, we need to be able to interact with empathy and respectful discernment for perspectives that differ from ours. Cross-cultural experiences help us learn to be students of our own culture and of another person's culture. Not everything in one's own culture, or another culture, should be accepted blindly. Cross-cultural mentoring experiences can help you learn how to formulate and express Christian theology with appropriate engagement in diverse contexts.

Some of you reading this book have come to a new country to study in a culture different from your own. For others, your racial background is different from the predominant racial background on campus. For others, you may have an opportunity to be mentored by a teacher or a pastor who is culturally or racially different from you.

In a cross-cultural mentoring situation, time needs to be set aside to discuss areas where there may be cross-cultural misunderstandings. This is especially true in the areas of perception, communication, and values. For example, does one person's culture value the individual over the collective or the collective over the individual? Is the person rewarded for taking risks or for avoiding risks in his or her culture? Is the greater cultural value to keep tradition or to break tradition? What about the role of power in relationships in his or her culture? Does a person's culture stress hierarchy in roles or equality in roles? Is a person's role in the natural and social world to master it or to be in harmony with it?[21]

Of course, the qualities of a mentoring relationship that have already been discussed—actively teaching and serving as a resource person, attentively teaching, creating an environment of trust, and loving courageously—are key to all mentoring relationships, including cross-cultural ones. But in addition to these foundational issues, it is important in a cross-cultural relationship for both you and your mentor to talk about how to develop a working knowledge of and appreciation for the other's culture. Both of you need to come to terms with your own cultural bias and to read the other person's culture as well. If English is not your or your mentor's native language, constantly check for understanding to make sure the communication is clear.[22]

As a word of warning, do not try to place the other person into a fixed cultural lens. We all know that stereotypes are bad, but we also have to admit that it is easy to use the same cultural lens on every person from a particular culture. We can fall into the trap of thinking, "In my experiences, all Chinese students . . ." or "I know that all African American churches are like . . ." This happens to the best of us. The key is to become a student of both culture and of the other person's uniqueness within an atmosphere of trust.

Finding a Beneficial Internship Site

The first two ingredients of our internship recipe, you as a proactive intern and your mentor providing caring support, have been added to the healthy internship mix. The remaining foundational ingredient is the actual internship site.

A word of clarification is needed here as well. At some schools, students have little choice as to when or where they participate in the internship because of the school's course sequencing. At other schools, the school or the denomination takes the primary role in placing the intern at a predetermined internship site. As I have already mentioned, the individual student at our school selects his or her own internship site and mentor based on their degree track. Nevertheless, just as particular mentoring qualities are vital for success no matter the mentor selection process, the internship site is also essential for a successful experience. As much as you are able to have a say in your internship placement, use these principles to guide your decision:

1. School and denominational requirements
2. Learning potential
3. Time requirement
4. Monetary compensation

Not all internship sites are created equal and not every great internship site is great for every student. To find the best internship site for you, you need to discover what you want to get out of the internship experience. This is your internship and no one else's internship. Do not take the first internship that comes along. The more options you investigate, the greater the likelihood that you will end up with an internship that fits who you are and what you are looking for.

No matter what process your school uses in internship site selection, the first step is to talk with the academic instructor who oversees the internship program at your school. Contacting your school early in your academic career will help ensure that you will have both an internship that is personally fulfilling and an internship that meets the school's academic (and possibly denominational) requirements. Probably better than anyone else, this academic instructor will know of the opportunities available and which site would be the best fit for you. Many times the academic instructor will have already established relationships with the on-site supervisors.

Besides your academic instructor, you also will want to talk with your peers about their past internship experiences. Some of the students nearing graduation have been down the same road you are now journeying on. They can offer valuable feedback on potential internship sites, as well as warnings of internship sites to avoid if possible. Keep in mind, however, that their experiences might not match your potential experiences. So while one student might have hated his or her term in a Clinical Pastoral Education (CPE) program at a local hospital, you might love the very same experience. So balance the advice of other students with the wisdom of the school's officials and your own uniqueness.

Ultimately, you are responsible for investigating and pursuing the internship options available to you. Invest some time early in your academic career looking at options and requirements. You cannot wait until the last minute to find an internship. You need to clarify your goals for obtaining an internship and decide what kind of internship you want to have.

At the same time, be realistic. Internships require a huge commitment of your time and energy. You need to know ahead of time the limitations you face. These can include family situations, transportation difficulties, financial considerations, time availability, lack of credit opportunities, and school internship requirements. Make sure that you are being wise in your internship selection. So, while the year-long internship in Hawaii might sound great in your imagination, can you realistically participate in it compared to a local internship?

Internship Site Selection Questions

To get you started, here are some general questions to spark the investigation process for you.

WHAT ARE THE SCHOOL'S AND DENOMINATION'S REQUIREMENTS FOR AN APPROVED INTERNSHIP?

In addition to meeting your school's requirements, if you are seeking ordination within a denomination, you need to coordinate your plans with denominational requirements for your internship experience. How many hours do you have to serve in an internship? How long is the internship? One summer? One semester? One year? Is a Clinical Pastoral Education (CPE) experience required? Is a cross-cultural experience required? Is a youth or children's experience required?

Do not assume that any and every internship opportunity you hear about on campus or from other people will qualify as an official internship for your degree plan. At this early stage, speaking to the academic instructor who oversees internships at your school is vital for you to do. I know from personal experience that this person will appreciate you coming by early in your selection process instead of trying to convince him or her that the youth ministry job you have already signed up for will be the perfect internship for you.

WHAT LEARNING POTENTIAL DOES EACH SITE HAVE?

Second, examine the learning potential at the internship site. Start by looking at your past experiences and training. What previous field experience have you had? For example, if you have already done an internship as a youth minister while in college, you might want to try something different in seminary—if you are allowed to by the school. Look at the classes you have already taken to make sure you have adequate classroom preparation for the internship. For example, if you have not had any preaching classes yet, you might not want to take an internship where the primary role is preaching each week.

Ask yourself if this internship opportunity will give you a chance to apply and test the education you have received. If you are training at school for one particular ministry area (for example, music ministry, pastoral ministry, chaplaincy) and the internship has nothing to do with that ministry area, you may need to consider if that internship is a wise choice. While serving as a children's minister for a semester might be a good and humbling learning experience in servanthood, will it help you in the long term if you are preparing to be a senior pastor someday? What about the missions candidate who never goes to another country to serve? That internship site decision does not seem to be in the student's best interest.

An internship opportunity at the megachurch or in another part of the country might sound glamorous and exciting, but ask yourself if this internship opportunity provides the significant on-the-job training you need. A paid internship opportunity might help pay the bills, but ask if this internship is really going to help you in the long run with your developmental goals. Does this internship provide a setting where appropriate resources are available for you to meet your developmental goals? Does this internship opportunity harmonize with your vocational intent? Does this internship match your giftedness, your passions, and your future ministry contexts—for example, a rural church setting, an urban church setting, a cross-cultural setting, or a nonprofit organizational setting? Does this internship provide opportunities to develop leadership and decision-making skills? And does this internship provide occasions for theological reflection?

HOW MUCH TIME IS REQUIRED?

A third area to consider is the time requirement. Again, depending on your school and denominational requirements, an internship can range from a few hours a week while you are concurrently taking classes on campus (concurrent placement) to a year-long internship in a full-time pastoral setting (block placement). Let me take a few moments to explain the differences.

Concurrent Placement

Concurrent placement refers to serving in a ministry setting part time (around ten hours a week) during the school year while attending classes full time. For example, this could be the student who works as a part-time youth minister at a local church while going to school full time. One advantage of concurrent placement is that integration of the classroom experience with ministry experience occurs. Most likely, what you are learning on Thursday in class, you are using on Sunday at the church. Another advantage is that, for better or for worse, you are forced to learn time-management skills because you have to balance school life and ministry life.

Finally, concurrent placement gives you the advantage of seeing ministry develop over a long-term period. With concurrent placement, you have an entire year or maybe longer to see ministry develop and to build relationships. Many times in local concurrent placements, the opportunities to minister continue long after the official internship has ended.

Nevertheless, with these advantages are disadvantages as well. Trying to balance school and an internship is stressful on both ends. When you are trying to do both things at the same time, you will possibly feel guilty because of time limitations. For instance, if you serve as a part-time youth minister at a local church, you will want to spend more time with the kids, but you cannot because of school demands. At the same time, you will want to focus more on your academic work but will feel pulled by the demands of the internship.

Another disadvantage of this type of concurrent placement is that you might not feel fully integrated with the ministry staff where you are serving. Unlike the full-time staff, you will not be able to attend all of the meetings because of your class schedule. You might miss out on planning days or certain discussions because you are not present at the ministry location during the week.

Block Placement
Block placement involves serving full time in a ministry setting during a block of time—a summer, a semester, or even a year—and not attending classes during this time. While concurrent placement involves serving a local church, you might, in a block placement, work at a local church or travel to another part of the country to serve in a full-time capacity.

The advantage of block placement is full ministry immersion. For those weeks and months of the internship, you are fully engaged in ministry at the internship site. Unlike the concurrent placement, you do not have to juggle classes and the internship. With block placement, you have freedom from educational demands. And in a block placement you will have a better opportunity for integration with the ministry staff where you are serving.

However, as with concurrent placement, block placement has its disadvantages. One is detachment of the academic life from the ministry experience. Unlike the concurrent placement where the potential exists for immediate application of what you have just learned in class, a block placement situation lacks that immediacy. Another disadvantage is that block placement is logistically more difficult to set up, especially if you are a married student. You have to ask yourself if you will be able to support yourself and your family financially if you take a full-time internship. If the internship site for the block placement is out of town, how will you deal with moving your family for the summer or for the year? And once the block placement internship is over, how do you transition back into the normal school routine?

So Which Is Best?

Do I recommend a concurrent or a block placement? Well, it depends. Some of it depends on your school's and your denomination's requirements. For your degree or for your ordination, you might be required to do either a concurrent placement *or* a block placement, or perhaps a concurrent placement *and* a block placement. So, always check your school requirements first. Your internship instructor will be able to tell you exactly what is required.

But if you have the freedom to choose one setting or another, then the decision sometimes depends on your personality. Can you juggle multiple demands simultaneously or do you prefer to concentrate on one thing at a time?

The decision may also depend on finances. Can you afford to take a summer or a semester off from work to pursue a block placement internship opportunity? Likewise, can you afford to fulfill a concurrent placement internship opportunity and pay your bills?

The decision may also depend on your family situation. Does your husband or wife want to move across the country for the summer? Do you have small kids?

The decision may also depend on the opportunities. If you want to do a media internship in the movie industry but are going to a seminary in the Midwest, you will probably need to go to California or New York to experience a beneficial internship. If you want to be a military chaplain, Uncle Sam will probably tell you where you will do your internship. If your passion is for missions, you will probably want to go to a mission field in another country for the summer or the year to get a better perspective of what long-term ministry looks and feels like.

I have seen both block placements and concurrent placements work fantastically. As I related in my story at the beginning of this book, I did a nine-month internship one thousand miles away from my home and school. That year I took off from school was one of the most important decisions I ever made. At the same time, I have personally supervised interns who have had life-changing experiences in a concurrent internship placement.

Therefore, as I said, it depends. I encourage you to develop a discerning heart and to seek the wisdom of others in helping you arrive at your decision. But no matter the format, all internships involve your time. Because time is a valuable commodity, do not take the time element of an internship lightly. You need to honestly ask yourself how much time you can realistically allocate to this internship opportunity.

The last thing you want to do is get all excited about serving in an internship opportunity only to realize a couple of weeks into it that you have bitten off more than you can chew. This usually happens to my students in October and February each year, when the first round of tests hits in the classroom.

As Jesus told his followers, "For which of you, desiring to build a tower, does not first sit down and count the cost, whether he has enough to complete it? Otherwise, when he has laid a foundation and is not able to finish, all who see it begin to mock him, saying, 'This man began to build and was not able to finish'" (Luke 14:28-30).

WHAT MONETARY COMPENSATION DOES THE SITE OFFER?

A natural question in dealing with internship site selection is the question of compensation. Money should never be the deciding factor in whether to take an internship position or not, but you do have financial obligations to meet. Do you need your travel, education, or other expenses covered by a paid internship? Does the internship opportunity meet your needs for compensation or will you also have to work another job in order to pay your bills?

At the same time, do not overlook volunteer or low-paying internship positions. Do not let pride get in the way of educational potential. Many times these smaller settings are just what are needed for your development.[23]

Are You Ready to Cook?

Now you have considered the ingredients necessary to start a great internship. If you are proactive in seeking your internship opportunities, if you are seeking a caring mentor to share the journey with, and if you are hunting for a beneficial internship site, you are well on the way to cooking up the recipe for internship success. Remember, however, that you cannot guarantee the success of your internship. Even the souffles made by the best chefs fall now and then. All you can humanly do is create the environment for the Holy Spirit to work in your life to bring about life change. However, if the recipe is followed, success is much more likely than failure.

Questions for Reflection

1. On a scale of 1 to 5 (1 meaning strongly disagree and 5 meaning strongly agree), rate yourself on the following indicators of being a proactive intern:

   1 2 3 4 5 I am a self-motivated person in my education.
   1 2 3 4 5 I take personal ownership in my educational development.
   1 2 3 4 5 I do not procrastinate in school or in life.
   1 2 3 4 5 I am teachable.
   1 2 3 4 5 I am eager to learn.
   1 2 3 4 5 I can identify some areas of growth in my past.
   1 2 3 4 5 I can identify some areas in my life where growth is needed.

2. Now, in a journal, write about times when you have demonstrated the traits or habits identified above, or failed to demonstrate them. What did you learn about yourself from the experience?
3. Based on what you have learned about yourself through journaling and self-assessment, what will you do the same or differently to be a proactive intern? What steps do you need to take this semester?
4. Outside of your immediate family, who is a person who has had a significant impact in your life and development? What were the qualities of that person? What made his or her impact so significant in your life?
5. Review the section "Working alongside a Caring Mentor," pages 41–58, and make a checklist of qualities and characteristics you will look for in a mentor. Identify

three that are most important to you and your internship experience. Keep the list in a place where you can refer to it in conversations about potential internship sites.

6. Have you ever had a close relationship with a person of a different culture? If so, what did you learn about yourself and about that person? How could you benefit from more cross-cultural exposure?

7. Have you secured an internship site? If so, what attracted you to that location? If not, what things are you looking for in an internship site?

8. Use this list to help you evaluate possible internship sites and potential mentors. Respond to each of the questions below, using a scale of 1 to 5 (1 meaning strongly disagree and 5 meaning strongly agree).

1 2 3 4 5   This site meets my school's requirements for an internship site.

1 2 3 4 5   This site meets my denomination's requirements for an internship site.

1 2 3 4 5   This site provides the specific learning potential I need for my ministry preparation.

1 2 3 4 5   I can meet the time requirements this internship site demands.

1 2 3 4 5   I am satisfied with the monetary compensation this internship site provides.

1 2 3 4 5   This site provides adequate supervision from an on-site mentor.

1 2 3 4 5   The mentor at this site is able to teach me the knowledge, skills, and values I need for my ministry preparation.

1 2 3 4 5   The mentor demonstrates attentive listening skills.

1 2 3 4 5   The mentor is able to create an environment of trust at the internship site.

1 2 3 4 5   The mentor demonstrates courageous love.

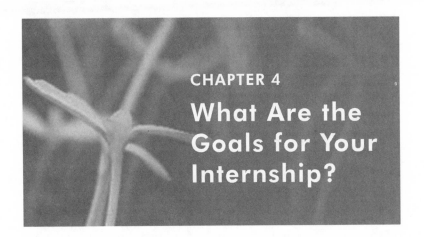

CHAPTER 4

What Are the Goals for Your Internship?

AS I WRITE THIS BOOK, MY DAUGHTER IS GETTING READY to enter middle school. She is eleven, so my wife and I figure that we have only seven more summers with her before she goes off to college. We were shocked when we realized that we are halfway to becoming empty nesters! Where did the time go?

My wife and I have fond memories from our own childhoods of family driving-vacations where we would load up the station wagon (I am not sure my daughter knows what a station wagon is!), get up at four o'clock in the morning, and head off on a marathon drive across the United States. My wife and I now have a mythic quest to take our daughter to one iconic U.S. vacation spot each summer for the next seven summers—a sort of a twenty-first-century version of our own growing up years (minus the station wagon). Because of this quest, we have a road atlas that we use to highlight our destinations. Whenever the topic of summer vacation is brought up, the map comes out and plans are made.

The first step in planning that vacation is asking, "Where do we want to go this year?" Every trip needs to have a destination. It sounds obvious, but one has to know where he or she is going to figure out how to get there. The clearer you are about where you are heading and how you are going to get there, the quicker you will be in reaching your destination and the fewer complications you will encounter along the way. With fuzzy goals or, worse, no goals, the vacation ends up being a car that has run out of gas and is sitting on the side of the road on the way to nowhere.

Your Goals Are Your Destinations

The same need for direction is true with an internship. If you are following the recipe described in the last chapter (a proactive intern, a caring mentor, and a beneficial internship site), you are off to a great start. But where are you going with the internship? Good intentions are not enough to guarantee a quality learning experience. The goals of an internship serve as the destinations for the internship. Goals keep you on track in your development. Through goal setting, focus enters into the internship.

Your school or your denomination most likely has a specific document with a template for goal development for you to complete at the start of your internship. These formal goals will provide the structure for your relationships and experiences during the internship, answering the question, "How do I best prepare for my ministry or range of ministries?" Without these well-defined goals, relationships and experiences in your internship can lose their focus and purpose, which is your growth.

The central question for goal setting is what you need in your professional and spiritual development to fulfill the ministry role for which God has designed you. So, building on the goal-setting material your school provides, how do you determine what your goals might be? The sources for your goals can come from

- Ministry area audits provided in this book and those provided by your school or denomination;
- Conversations with your mentor;

- Conversations with the lay committee or ministry participants at your internship site;
- Conversations with ministry professionals in your anticipated ministry area to discover the knowledge and skills needed;
- Discovering areas of needed growth uncovered in your classes and reading;
- Discovering areas of needed growth uncovered in previous ministry or employment experiences;
- Input from family and friends.

Developing Character and Ministry Competencies

While I wish it were otherwise, no comprehensive list of ministry goal areas that every student should focus on in his or her internship exists. Ministry needs vary from setting to setting (urban church, rural church, small church, large church, African American church, Asian American church, Hispanic church, and so on), from tradition to tradition (Baptist, Episcopal, Presbyterian, Catholic, Charismatic, Eastern Orthodox, Lutheran, Methodist, and so on), and from role to role (senior pastor, associate pastor, youth pastor, children's pastor, women's pastor, chaplain, church planter, missionary, and so on). While some ministry skills can be universally applied, other skills are more specialized.

Internship goals should address both developing character and developing ministry competencies, remembering that the ultimate objective for any internship is the development of the whole person. Areas of development can include the following: family and marriage, financial, personal, physical, professional, social, or spiritual. The following sections include key questions and competencies you may want to consider when developing your goals.

Character: Who You Need to Be

An authentic development plan needs to include your character. The character question is "Who do you need to be?" *Being* (character) always must precede *doing* (tasks and skills). This is why the scriptural qualifications for leadership found in 1 Timothy 3 and Titus 1 focus so heavily on the leader's character, not the leader's skills or abilities. The heart of leadership is the leader's heart. A leader's character must be above reproach.

You can have an engaging personality, but personality without character will only get you so far in ministry. You can be a driven person with a clear vision for the future, but without the foundation of character you can easily drive off the road. You can be passionate about what you are doing, but without the light of character those passions can also blind you. You can be the smartest student in your class, but good grades will never make up for a lack of character.[1]

In their studies in leadership over the last twenty years, researchers James Kouzes and Barry Posner have found consistently that people choose to follow leaders who are honest (88 percent of respondents), forward thinking (71 percent of respondents), competent (66 percent of respondents), and inspiring (65 percent of respondents).[2] Kouzes and Posner explain,

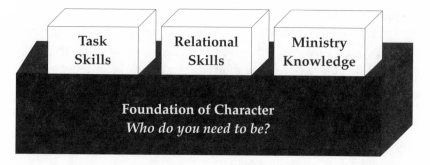

Figure 4.1. Foundation of Character in Leadership

In almost every survey we've conducted, honesty has been selected more often than any other leadership characteristic; overall, it emerges as the single most important ingredient in the leader-constituent relationship. . . . If people anywhere are to willingly follow someone—whether it be into battle or into the boardroom, the front office or the front lines—they first want to assure themselves that the person is worthy of their trust. They want to know that the person is truthful, ethical, and principled. . . . Credibility is the foundation of leadership.[3]

Leadership development is about the whole person, not only the how-to of leadership. In reality, the how-to part is much easier than character development. A good internship and mentoring relationship can create healthy leaders of character. A key goal of your internship should be to examine your spiritual life to discover your character blind spots and to encourage you to begin dealing with them before they become a serious problem later.

Character goals can include any of the following:

- Love
- Joy
- Peace
- Patience
- Kindness
- Goodness
- Faithfulness
- Gentleness
- Self-Control

Ministry Competencies

Competence development is what most people think of when they consider an internship. Competence is seen as having the underlying skills, qualities, abilities, knowledge, and work habits that characterize successful individuals in the workplace or in a particular field. Competence forces schools to ask what graduates should know, be able to do, and value.

An internship is the ideal learning opportunity for you to gain an understanding of the areas of competence needed for a specific career field and for you to assess areas of competence that need to be improved. An internship is also the best way to develop transferable transformational leadership skills vital to any setting.

For example, a student who wants to be a senior pastor of a church needs to know how to do the pastoral tasks of preaching, conducting weddings and funerals, handling budgets, and so forth. The same student needs to grasp broader leadership

Figure 4.2: Ministry Competency Goals

skills as well, such as vision casting and empowering followers. A healthy internship for this student would allow the student to have exposure to many of these competencies.

A balanced internship gives you an advantage. An internship can act as a catalytic converter, speeding up the learning process by eliminating some of the trial and error in competence building that a graduating student usually faces once he or she is on the job. With growth in a competency area, you gain confidence in transitioning into the post-school professional world.

Some of the competencies you need to learn fall into the categories of task skills, relational skills, and ministry knowledge. Let me briefly unpack each of these.

TASK-SKILL GOALS: HOW YOU DO THE WORK

When thinking about setting goals in an internship, task-skill goals are usually the ones that come to mind. Each vocational track—senior pastor, missionary, Christian education, chaplaincy, teaching, children's ministry—at school has certain tasks associated with that ministry area.

Examples of task skills include any of the following:

- Organizing a church's leadership retreat
- Developing a visitor follow-up program for a church
- Grading academic papers for a professor
- Planning a budget
- Developing a vision statement for a ministry
- Working with a board of elders at a church
- Organizing a publicity plan for a ministry
- Performing a wedding
- Performing a baptism
- Making hospital visits
- Using PowerPoint
- Writing a book review for a scholarly journal

- Working with a mission agency

All of these tasks focus on how you do the work.

RELATIONAL SKILL GOALS: HOW TO WORK WELL WITH PEOPLE

By its very nature, leadership is relational. A leader is not a leader unless other people are involved. A leader cannot lead in a people vacuum. Relational skill goals focus on working well with people. Most students find this one of the most rewarding development areas during their internship.

Relational skill goals include any of the following:

- Active listening
- Encouraging
- Networking
- Resolving conflict
- Risk taking
- Problem solving
- Confronting
- Trust building
- Team or community building
- Inspiring or motivating
- Consensus building
- Recruiting
- Mentoring or modeling
- Counseling
- Hiring and firing
- Conducting meetings
- Delegating

MINISTRY-KNOWLEDGE GOALS: WHAT YOU NEED TO KNOW

One of the main reasons you are attending Bible college or seminary is probably to expand your knowledge in the Bible and theology. Expanding your knowledge base in the ministry context is also important. This area focuses on the ministry knowledge question, "What do you need to know?"

The difference between a ministry-knowledge goal and the first two goal areas (task skills and relational skills) is subtle. A ministry-knowledge goal involves cognitive content as it relates to ministry, not necessarily action-based learning. A ministry-knowledge goal is something that you need to *know* for your vocational setting but that you probably will not actually *do* during the internship. The following examples illustrate the main difference between a ministry-knowledge goal and a task-skill goal.

A pastoral student might determine that he needs to know how to work with a church's board of elders. While this student will probably not have an opportunity to actually lead (task-skill goal) an elder board meeting during the scope of the internship, this student can identify a ministry-knowledge goal of attending an elder board meeting, interviewing an elder at the church, or reading a book about working with leadership boards.

An academic teaching student might determine that she needs to know how to publish a scholarly journal article. While this student will probably not have an opportunity to actually write and publish (task-skill goal) a journal article during the scope of the internship, this student can identify a ministry-knowledge goal of interviewing an editor of a scholarly journal, assisting her professor in writing a book review, or reviewing journal articles for her professor.

A Christian education student might determine that she needs to know how to plan a church budget. While this student will probably not have an opportunity to plan (task-skill goal) an entire church's budget, this student can identify a ministry-knowledge goal of sitting in on a church budget meeting or interviewing the church's executive pastor to discuss budget planning.

A pastoral student might determine that he needs to know how to conduct a funeral. While this student will probably not have an opportunity to conduct (task-skill goal) a funeral, this student can identify a ministry-knowledge goal of observing her ministry mentor conduct a funeral or interviewing a funeral home director.

COMPETENCIES CHECKLISTS

In appendix B and appendix C of this book, you will find two lists of ministry competencies we use at Dallas Theological Seminary to guide students and mentors in ministry-competency goal development. Appendix B describes general ministry leadership competencies that we have concluded apply to all leaders in all ministry settings. The competencies on this list come from a variety of transformational leadership and emotional intelligence sources.[4] While this list is in no way exhaustive, it at least provides a starting point. Your school or denomination may have a similar list of competencies.

The second list, appendix C, offers more setting-specific ministry competencies, based on ministry audiences and ministry contexts.[5] Again, your school or denomination may have a similar list.

As you consider goals that come out of your developmental needs, your mentor can be of help, particularly in the area of bringing specificity and developmental focus to the goals. As I have noted previously in this book, individuals in addition to your mentor may be involved in providing oversight and direction during the internship. Some schools and denominations require the intern to have a lay committee, an advisory council, or ministry consultants on-site in addition to the mentor. Members of such a group play the same key role as the mentor. Goal setting is a work in progress that takes time as you and your mentor move your goals from the general to the specific.

For example, you might have a general goal of becoming a better teacher. This is a broad and fuzzy goal. Your mentor, however, can help you refine this goal to become more manageable. As a result of this mentoring guidance, your goal might be refined to specify teaching methods (confidence in speaking in front of a large audience, better small group facilitation skills, creative use of multimedia, or framing better discussion questions) or maybe audience contexts (learning how to teach older adults, teenagers, or young children). So, instead of the broad goal, "I want to be a better teacher," the goal is honed to read, "I want to learn how to incorporate small group exercises into the youth Bible studies I lead." With the more refined goal (using behavioral language), the end target becomes clearer and therefore reachable.[6]

Besides helping with initial goal setting, your mentor can assist you in adjusting your goals along the way. Goals are moveable targets—that is, you and your mentor can adapt them as the internship environment, your personal life, or your thinking about your developmental goals changes.[7] If the goals set six months ago are no longer valid, do not continue down a path you have no desire to follow. You and your mentor always need to be open to reevaluating the goals of the internship and making adjustments accordingly.

So, let us use as an illustration teaching and goal setting for a youth ministry internship. During your internship, you begin to counsel one of the parents of a high school student about the couple's marital problems. Due to the new situation thrust upon you and perceiving the need to improve your counseling skills, you and your mentor decide to shift some goals to improving your counseling skills or to explore the marital resources found in the local community.

Setting Challenging and Realistic Goals

As you and your mentor begin to identify and consider character and competency goals for your internship, aim to include goals that will challenge you yet are realistic enough to achieve.

Challenging Goals

A reality of life is that we need to be stretched in order to grow. By nature, we tend to go through life thinking and acting in ways that are comfortable and customary to us. As long as our circumstances are not altered, we feel no need to move out of our comfort zone. If our assumptions and strengths worked in the past, we rationalize that they should be sufficient for the future. But as a result, we have not allowed ourselves room for growth.[8]

But the challenges of life are where leadership skills are developed. The lackluster and the routine do not help us cultivate new skills and abilities. The only way to mature is to be stretched, to take chances to test ourselves against new and difficult tasks. Experiences full of personal challenge are many times the best teachers.[9] Challenges create tension or disequilibrium, causing us to consider the validity of our skills, values, and approaches. Learning takes place when these challenges force us to reconcile the differences and when we have to evaluate your old ways of thinking.[10]

The Center for Creative Leadership, a leadership educational and research organization based in Greensboro, North Carolina, talks about four sources of challenge in leadership development: novelty, difficult goals, conflict, and hardship.[11] Let me briefly define each of these and give an example for each one.

NOVELTY
Novelty is defined by Ellen Van Velsor and Cynthia McCauley as those new experiences where you are required to use new skills or to develop new ways of understanding yourself in relation to others.[12] So a novel goal for you could be serving in a familiar

Figure 4.3. Sources of Challenge

role, maybe as a youth minister, but at a different church for a semester. Or novelty might come from serving in a familiar role, maybe as a camp counselor, but in a cross-cultural setting. Possibly the novelty comes from applying a skill you have learned in class to a real-life setting—for example, using PowerPoint for the first time in a class you teach at the church.

DIFFICULT GOALS

Van Velsor and McCauley define difficult goals as goals that force you to work harder than you normally would or goals that result in you discovering that just working harder in your comfortable manner is not enough. Instead of working harder, you have to work differently to reach the goal.[13] So, while you may have been a camp counselor before, maybe this summer you will be the camp director overseeing all of the camp counselors. While the skill set needed as a camp director includes some of the same skills needed as a camp counselor, you also have to learn additional skills. Recruitment, training, goal setting, vision casting, delegation, team building, communication, and conflict resolution all need to be developed for you to survive the summer as the camp director. If you treat the role of camp director in the same way as being a camp counselor you will have a very long summer ahead of you. Being a camp director means much more than being a glorified camp counselor.

CONFLICT

If viewed as a means of development, experiencing conflict and dealing effectively with it can be a fantastic teaching tool in your life. Whether the conflict is with a person or a group, you have to learn how to understand the other perspective and how to differentiate that point of view from your own. In dealing with conflict, you might even discover that you need to reshape your own point of view.[14]

The idea is not for you to have as one of your goals, "I will have a vicious personal conflict with a coworker and will learn from the experience." However, when you are faced with a conflict you are having with a coworker or a participant at the internship site, you and your mentor need to look at the learning potential presented in the conflict.

HARDSHIP

As with conflict, hardship is not likely to be included on your goal development sheet. But the reality of life is that hardship happens. Hardships include coming to terms with the loss of a loved one, dealing with your own mistakes or failure at a task, or wrestling with disappointment with a person or a situation. Times of hardship, when things do not go according to your well-laid plans, create bewilderment and kindle a search for new meaning and understanding. These are the times when you come to terms with your own shortcomings and humanity. Hardships also teach people how to persevere and cope with difficult situations.[15] The lessons learned from hardship are sometimes the lessons that will never be learned any other way.[16] During times of hardship, the support of a caring mentor becomes all the more important.

Challenging Goals  Realistic Goals

Figure 4.4. Tension of Challenging Goals and Realistic Goals

An internship serves as the gym for the ministerial muscles to be built. You will only develop when you are challenged outside of your comfort zone. Do not set goals too low. For example, if you have been teaching seventh grade Sunday school for the last five years, one of your goals should not be to teach a seventh grade Sunday school class. You have mastered this experience. But what if you are asked to preach your first "real" sermon in front of the entire church? Once the initial terror of speaking in front of large groups subsides, you will have a fantastic opportunity to put your classroom instruction into real-life practice.

Realistic Goals

The goal development coin has another side. At this stage, you might develop dozens of potential goals. Do not try to tackle too many goals, but instead prioritize the most crucial areas on which to focus. For example, is the goal realistic, considering your resources of time, money, and so forth, during your academic studies? Although the internship needs to challenge you, you will only get frustrated if you have set unrealistic goals.

Do not expect everything in the internship to come together overnight. Mentoring takes time. Growth, like anything significant, takes time. While the "blinding flash of insight or epiphany on the mountaintop [is] always possible," for most of us change is "more like agriculture than rocket science."[17]

The key is to strike the right balance between challenge and realism. A goal needs enough challenge to stretch your learning.

But if a goal requires too much stretching, you can become overwhelmed, defensive, discouraged, or burned out.[18]

How can you whittle down your many possible goals to a reasonable number? Here are some questions to ask when appraising your developmental goals:

1. What are you motivated to work on?
2. How much challenge can you add to your current responsibilities?
3. What can you afford not to address?
4. What goals will offer the greatest advantage for your existing leadership strengths?
5. What does the feedback suggest you need to improve?
6. What do you feel is important?
7. What personal goals do you want to work on but do not want to disclose to others?[19]

Your Mentor's Role in Setting Goals

In the previous chapter, we explored the importance of the mentor creating an environment of trust for the internship. That trust is like a seedbed for your growth. An environment of trust and growth does not happen by accident. This environment needs to be designed so that you can be stretched in your ministry experiences but not beyond your abilities.

Mentors can be tempted to jump in too soon to solve a challenging situation for an intern. Your mentor needs to resist the temptation to rescue you too soon from the situation; at the same time, you need to be on guard not to expect your mentor to save you, to solve the problem for you. If your mentor steps in too soon, he or she can shortchange your experience by not allowing you to discover the answer yourself.[20]

When faced with a challenge, use it as an opportunity to try out the skills you have learned. Use your own problem-solving skills first (doing research, brainstorming, weighing your options) before defaulting to your mentor. Growth comes as a challenging situation forces you to reconcile that situation with what you bring to it.

Just as the responsibility of challenging you is one of your mentor's tasks, bringing the balance of realism is also the mentor's task. As a student, you are probably full of ideas and ready to conquer the world by next week. Most students try to accomplish everything in a single internship. What your mentor can do is to help focus your aims and set realistic goals.

Accomplishing Your Goals: Strategies and Measures

The reason for designing goals is ultimately to enhance your growth and preparation for the ministry you believe God has designed you to fulfill while at school and beyond. After you have mapped out your goals for internship, with the help of your mentor and others, design a specific *strategy* to accomplish each goal along with *measures* for each strategy. Your school might call this a learning agenda or a development plan; but no matter the name, the purpose is the same. A goal with no plan for how to reach the goal is ultimately useless.

Figure 4.5. Strategies for Goal Development

Strategies

If the goal is the destination on the map, the strategy is the route you plan to use to get to your destination.

Developing a strategy toward your individual goals will help you make the best use of the resources God gave you. This is especially true when it comes to your time. Even if you are serving at an internship site for an entire year, that year will be over before you know it. If you do not have a strategy in place for reaching each of your goals, you will find yourself at the end of the internship wondering where the time went and frustrated as you try to cram in all the experiences you wanted to have during the internship. I hear these comments all the time:

"I wanted to work on my spiritual discipline of prayer during the internship, but I was so busy that I never got around to focusing on it."

"My mentor and I talked about me sitting in on some of his premarital counseling sessions, but we both kind of forgot about it as the summer went along."

"I had the best of intentions to read that ministry book suggested by a member of my church, but life got too hectic during the internship."

So what does a development strategy look like? Let me give you a couple of examples. First, let us say that you have identified as one of your goals for the internship, "To deepen my personal worship time in my devotion to God." That is a wonderful goal for an internship, but how are you going to reach that goal? Your strategies may look like the following:

- Establish a consistent daily time for personal devotion (prayer and Bible study).
- Focus my personal devotional reading time on the attributes of God, focusing on the Psalms in particular.

- Increase Scripture memorization, focusing on verses that reveal God's character and attributes.
- Read John Ortberg's *The Life You've Always Wanted.*

This example illustrates how you took a good goal and put some clear action steps to guide you along the way.

Here is another one. Your goal might be, "To learn how to select or develop a Bible study curriculum for junior high students on Sunday mornings." Your strategies could be the following:

- Discuss curriculum development with my mentor.
- Review class notes and meet with the Christian education faculty on campus to discuss curriculum development.
- Meet with the youth pastor at my church to learn how the current curriculum was chosen for junior high students.
- Investigate what other youth ministers in the area are using for curriculum.

Again, the goal is clearly stated and definite strategies are in place to move in the direction of the goal.

One last one. Your goal is, "To learn how to work with an administrative assistant." Some of the strategies may be the following:

- Discuss with my mentor his or her understanding of the role of administrative assistants.
- Work weekly in the church office to learn firsthand about pastoral expectations and utilization of administrative assistants.
- Discuss with the administrative assistants different ways in which pastors and lay people work with them and any suggestions they have on how to capitalize on their services.

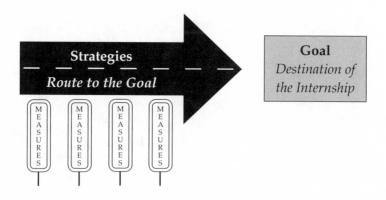

Figure 4.6. Measures for Goal Development

Write out steps you can take to reach your goals. Consulting with your mentor, decide if following a particular order would be beneficial. Put the actions into a logical sequence, answering who, what, and when. For your sake, being thorough is better than being skimpy.

Measures

Once the goal and the strategy to reach the goal are in place, the final question is, "How will I know when I am there?" In this final step, you, along with your mentor, decide the ways to measure progress toward the goal. If the goals are the destinations on the trip and the strategies are the route you are planning to take to the destination, the measures are the mile markers to determine how far you have traveled.

Most goals and strategies need *a target date,* so make sure to include this date in the measurement—for example, "I plan to preach my sermon by January." Also answer the "By whom?" question in the measurements, designating *who will hold you accountable* to complete your goal.

Using one of the examples discussed above, here is how

the goal, the strategies, and the measurements might all look together.

> **Goal:** To deepen my personal worship time in my devotion to God.

Strategies
- Establish a consistent daily time for personal devotion (prayer and Bible study).
- Focus my personal devotional reading time on the attributes of God, focusing on the Psalms in particular.
- Increase Scripture memorization, focusing on verses that reveal God's character and attributes.
- Read John Ortberg's *The Life You've Always Wanted.*

Measures
- Have a consistent personal devotion time of thirty uninterrupted minutes at least four days a week.
- Memorize one verse per week that focuses on the attributes of God and say it from memory to one person a week.
- Ask my mentor to hold me accountable to my personal devotional time on a weekly basis.
- Read *The Life You've Always Wanted* by January 1 and discuss the insights from that book with my mentor.

Appendix D includes more sample goals with corresponding sample strategies and measurements.

Are You Ready to Travel?

Summer is approaching as I write this, and in our house we are making plans for another one of our mythic quest vacations. In doing so, we have two options. One option is to jump in the car and head out. North? South? East? West? Who cares because we are on vacation. No map in hand. No hotel reservations. No searching on the Internet to find out what there is to do once we get there.

While the randomness of an "accidental tourist" method may result in a good time, I would much rather figure things out ahead of time. Trying to determine the basics of a trip, at a minimum, does not take the spontaneous away from our vacation, but with a little bit of effort on our part, we improve the chances of having a good time. In your internship, do not be an "accidental intern" who just hopes that things will work out. Can good things come from your internship if you do not plan for them? Yes they can, but simply taking time to do the basic things mentioned in this chapter will help a great deal in creating an environment for your potential growth and success.

Questions for Reflection

1. Think back to a time when you were challenged to do something that stretched you or something you had never done before. What was it? Did you succeed on the first try? When you did succeed, how did it feel?
2. What is one character goal you have for your internship?
3. What is one task-skill goal you have for your internship?
4. What is one relational skill goal you have your internship?
5. What is one ministry-knowledge goal you have for your internship?

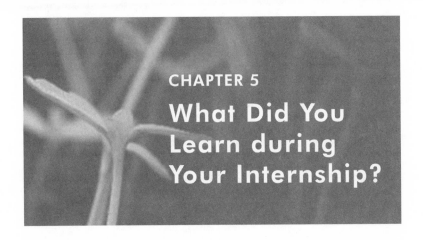

CHAPTER 5

What Did You Learn during Your Internship?

LAST CHRISTMAS, OUR FAMILY BOUGHT A JIGSAW PUZZLE to work on during the holidays, one with a picture of the *Peanuts* cartoon characters singing in the snow. When it came time to start working on the puzzle, putting Snoopy, Charlie Brown, Lucy, and the rest of the *Peanuts* gang together was the fairly easy part. Their puzzle pieces had distinctive color patterns and defined lines. After a little while, we had all of the characters fitted together.

The almost impossible part, however, was trying to fit the three hundred or so snow pieces together. It became a joke for us because every single piece was white, with no lines or any distinguishing marks to differentiate one piece from another. My wife, our daughter, and I set up an assembly line format to figure out the snow pieces. Even finding two snow puzzle pieces that fit together was a small victory. Once we conquered the puzzle, we were too proud of our triumph to take it apart, and therefore it stayed on our coffee table throughout the Christmas holidays.

In a way, internships are like putting together a puzzle. Prior to the start of your internship, you have learned a bit of theology in a class here, read a bit about ministry in a book there, experienced church life in your home church, and talked about many ministry issues with your peers. In a great internship setting, you have an opportunity to put these various puzzle pieces together to reveal a picture of what you look like in a ministry context. Self-awareness, skill development, theological understanding, and spiritual formation are like the individual groups of puzzle pieces with particular colors and patterns that are carefully connected to present a picture of who you are, what you do, how you understand faith, and how God is forming you.[1] Two of the ways these puzzle pieces come together in an internship are through learning from feedback and learning from theological reflection.

Pausing to Learn

Experience without feedback and reflection is not education. Life is so busy that time for receiving feedback and stopping to reflect does not often take place. This is especially true in Western culture, with its focus on the external and the active and its avoidance of the internal and the reflective.[2] Because of the commotion taking place on the outside, we have little opportunity to hear what is going on in the inside. We are always on the run but never have time to meet ourselves on the way. Only when you take time to receive feedback and to reflect on why you do what you do are you able to discover areas of growth. More important, when you take time to pause, you are able to see where God is present and active in your life.[3]

Research has shown that when we do not take the time to receive feedback and to reflect, we are destined to repeat the same old habits of yesterday to deal with the challenges of today and tomorrow.[4] In their study of leadership development among business executives, researchers Morgan McCall, Michael Lombardo, and Ann Morrison at the Center for Creative Leadership discovered that executives who learned from their failures examined both external and internal factors. The researchers found that successful learning took place only when a person recognized his or her limitations, accepted the limitations, and redirected his or her efforts after a failure. Only a difficult situation, "especially a wrenching trauma," required many of these leaders to deal with the reality of their personal and professional lives. But as noted by the research, "only the shovel-in-the-face kinds of events created a need for deep self-examination, and even then there were no guarantees."[5]

So, let us spend a little time on these two valuable skills—learning from feedback and learning through theological reflection.

Learning from Feedback

In stereotypical male fashion, I do not like going to the doctor. Please understand, I really like my doctor as a person, and I know that my doctor is on my side and wants to help me. I also know all of the health statistics concerning men who do not go to the doctor and the risk of undiagnosed illnesses. Nevertheless, I still do not go as often as I should.

Maybe the rolled paper on the examining table is the problem. Maybe it is the cold stethoscope. Maybe it is the shots. But no matter the reason, when it comes time for my regular checkup, I always have the excuse of "I am too busy. I cannot take time off from work." Or when I do feel sick, I have the excuse, "I know that I will get to feeling better if I can just rest for a couple of days." Even though I have all these excuses, I still go faithfully (with my wife's prodding) to see my doctor because I know I need regular evaluation of my overall health. I need to hear feedback from an outside source on what changes I need to make in my diet, my exercise routine, or my lifestyle. I plan on being around for a long, long time, so my doctor visits are important to me.

What is true for our health is also true for our leadership development. I need to have regular feedback on my leadership development just as I need a regular checkup with my doctor. And like the doctor visit, I sometimes avoid this needed assessment. A major goal of the internship is to help you evaluate your design, your direction, and your development in ministry. A key component of any healthy educational experience is feedback from other people.

Feedback Is Vital

Why is feedback so vital? One reason is the need for perspective. Outside feedback is critical to get a reality check, no matter if it is related to health or to leadership development. We all have blind spots. Having a formal, structured means of feedback allows you the opportunity to pause and to assess your growth and your effectiveness.

As a student, you have invested significant time and resources into your theological education. However, too many students leave school without ever asking the tough questions of life. The questions that you need to be asking yourself, especially throughout the internship process, are:

1. Am I on the right track? Is God still directing me in this particular ministry area?
2. Do I have the God-given giftings needed for this ministry area?
3. Do I have the passions and sense of joy needed for this ministry area?
4. Am I being confirmed by the community of faith in my ministry direction? What experiences support my conclusion?
5. What areas of my character or spiritual formation do I need to be working on?

6. What skills do I still need to learn in this ministry area?

With self-evaluation, informal feedback from others, and formal evaluation from others, it is paramount for you to wrestle with these questions. Seeking and receiving feedback is a part of being intentional in your own personal development. This process of intentional feedback in an internship is crucial in order for you to learn and grow from the ministry experience.

Scripture clearly calls us to seek the counsel and wisdom of others for our own benefit. That goes for both the words of encouragement and the words of correction. Consider the following: "If you listen to constructive criticism, you will be at home among the wise. If you reject discipline, you only harm yourself; but if you listen to correction, you grow in understanding" (Prov. 15:31-32 NLT). And "Unfriendly people care only about themselves; they lash out at common sense" (Prov. 18:1 NLT).

Feedback also invites accountability for growth. Feedback from other people provides you with information to measure whether you are making progress toward your developmental goals or if you are going in circles. Establishing goals and receiving feedback on those goals from other people can provide that extra motivation you may be looking for. With the right feedback from the right source (such as a caring mentor), you can eventually become self-correcting in some ways, understanding for yourself the needs you have and the assistance you desire. Under these conditions, you may be even more willing to put forth the effort you need to see change occur.[6]

Imagine that one of your goals for the internship was to overcome some of your shyness by being more confident in your conversations during church meetings. Early in your internship, you received encouragement from your mentor and others around you that you need to speak up more in staff meetings and committee meetings. You know that you have great ideas in your head during these meetings that you would like to share, but you have always been aware of other people's perceptions and concerned about saying the wrong thing. This is a tendency that you have struggled with most of your life. While not trying to change your basic personality, you have realized that in ministry you will need to speak up more. So, you ask for feedback on your speaking confidence from your mentor and other peers at the internship site throughout your time there.

Now fast-forward several months into the internship. With the gentle prodding of your mentor and with the feedback you have received from other people, you notice that speaking up in these meetings is coming a little easier as you progress through the internship. And the times when you had a great idea but did not share it in the meeting, your mentor reminds and encourages you to speak up next time. As a result of the encouragement you have received, you begin to notice when you are sliding back into the old habit of keeping silent when you have a good idea. As a result of this combination of feedback and self-correction, people comment at the end of your internship about the growth they have seen in your confidence about speaking up.

FORMAL AND INFORMAL FEEDBACK

Feedback can be both informal and formal. In part, *informal feedback* provides ongoing mirroring that occurs with other people during the course of ministry. This is feedback given promptly by either your mentor or a participant in your ministry in a situation where you have an opportunity to immediately put into practice or correct what is suggested by the feedback. Feedback in general needs to be continuous instead of only concentrated at the end of the internship. This allows you to receive the feedback while on the journey rather than waiting until the end of the journey for the formal evaluation.

Picture yourself starting out on a hike in the woods but only referring to the trail map at the start of the hike. With a visual image in your mind, you take off to enjoy a day in the woods. If the path is fairly easy, you may have a good chance of getting to your final campground for the night without referring to the trail map beyond that initial glance. But what if the trail is not clearly marked with signs along the way? What if your hike has a couple of forks in the trail that without the map, you would have to memorize in advance which turn to take and in what direction? What if you get out in the woods and all of the trees start looking alike? You would wonder, do I go right or left? When do I turn which way? At this point, it would be foolish to not refer to the trail map in your pocket.

Informal feedback is like referring to the trail map while you are still on the trail. Informal feedback can be a casual conversation or a well-timed word from your mentor, your lay committee, your peers, your ministry participants, your friends, or your family. Informal feedback may occur when you talk with a parishioner about how he or she thinks the children's ministry, for example, is going and you learn that some misinformation has been communicated between you and that parishioner. Informal feedback may occur when you talk with a high school student in the youth ministry, finding out that the student has not been coming to your teaching time because he or she has not connected with your teaching style. Informal feedback may occur when you talk with your ministry mentor or a member of your lay committee on a weekly basis, finding out that he or she thinks you may have overcommitted yourself on your latest project at church. Any interaction can become a source of informal feedback, if you are willing to listen.

Formal feedback (or evaluation), on the other hand, occurs periodically, such as at the midpoint or the conclusion of an internship. Returning to the trail map illustration, formal feedback occurs at the end of the hike, asking, "Did I make my final destination?" while informal feedback occurs during the hike as you recalibrate your route, asking, "Do I need to change the direction I am traveling to reach my final destination?"

Formal feedback paints a more complete picture of your assessment in an understandable form.[7] Formal feedback is more defined, thorough, and standardized and will likely occur during your final reflection session with your mentor or lay committee, but it can also occur during the middle of your internship. Your school, your church, your organization, or your denomination probably has a system in place that determines how often formal feedback occurs. A written assessment is likely to be part of your formal feedback. Some schools provide standardized assessments and other schools have in-house assessment tools for formal feedback. These can be either in a written form or in an oral form, such as an exit interview, or some combination.

No matter the form, if timely informal feedback is practiced throughout the internship, then the written evaluation at the conclusion of the internship should contain no surprises. Instead, the written evaluation only focuses and sums up what has already been said and experienced during the internship and the mentoring relationship.[8]

Feedback Is Scary

If feedback is so beneficial in a person's development, why do some people seem to avoid feedback? I know from firsthand familiarity that feedback is threatening. Allowing other people to speak truth on our lives is risky. In my selfishness, I only want to hear people say good things about me. The truth, though, is sometimes hurtful and uncomfortable.

When I see my doctor for a physical exam, my blood is drawn for testing—not a fun experience. Once the blood work is back from the lab, I may learn that my cholesterol is too high—not a pleasant conversation. However, I need to hear the truth about the results of my blood tests so that I can make changes in my diet and exercise. In both medicine and in life, healing power only comes through pain; when we are able to "tolerate the discomfort of the truth," we can also experience the benefit of health and growth in our life.[9]

Wanting to hear nothing but applause from other people is normal. Moreover, it is only natural for most mentors to want to give you only praise. However, if all you ever hear is the good and never hear where the areas of improvement are, does it really do you any good in the end? What is important is your openness to the process and your desire to look critically at your life and actions.[10]

Earlier in the book I described the concept of courageous love. One of the marks of a good mentor is a man or woman who loves courageously. A mentor has the needed perspective to look into your life and ministry, seeing where the gaps are and where God is at work. A mentor must be relational, empowering you in a safe but challenging environment where he or she is able to speak lovingly and courageously to you to correct imbalances. This requires patience from the mentor, knowing that change does not occur overnight.

360-DEGREE FEEDBACK

The ideal feedback situation is feedback from multiple sources. Business leaders call this 360-degree feedback, where you hear from the people who surround you in your particular context. Hearing these voices allows you to see "a panorama of perceptions, presenting a more complete picture than that afforded by any one group."[11] A major benefit of your internship is discovering how others perceive you. For some students, this is the first time in their life they have taken an objective look at their strengths and areas for improvement. Sometimes your self-perception and the perception of others can be far apart. This disequilibrium can become one of the greatest potential sources of growth in your life.

Disequilibrium works both ways, revealing both areas of undiscovered strengths and areas of undiscovered weaknesses, which present opportunities for growth. Let me illustrate both aspects. First, imagine you have been serving as a pastoral intern at a local church for the past year. During that year, you have especially enjoyed the teaching opportunities you have had in a weekly theology class sponsored by the church but have not found a real sense of joy in many of the other pastoral duties common to the ministry you are entering. You love the preparation time for teaching the theology class each week, diving into the Greek and Hebrew nuances of the biblical text you are studying with great passion. People in your class appreciate the extra effort you put into your weekly handouts, saying that your handouts and class lectures help to explain difficult theological issues. So, what if the people in the class asked you, "Have you ever thought about getting your PhD and teaching at a Bible college?" While you had never thought about that option before, your world of possibilities has just been opened by this insightful question by people who have sat under your teaching. This is the power of disequilibrium, in one sense.

Now, let me illustrate the other sense of disequilibrium. Imagine you are that same pastoral intern. In focusing on your development in sermon delivery, a member of your lay committee or another member of the congregation says, "Great job on your sermon, but you seemed really nervous when you were preaching on Sunday. In your sermon, you said 'umm' and 'you know' numerous times. Next week, can the pastor and I spend some time talking about some tips for sermon delivery? Would that be OK?" In this example, you hear the truth about your nervous habit of saying "umm" and "you know," but you also received an offer to help you improve in that area. The focus of feedback in an internship is to help you learn and grow. To be beneficial, the feedback needs to aim at discoveries and improvements you can do something about.

Those people who have directly experienced your leadership and ministry should be the primary providers of feedback. Rumors and secondhand knowledge are not good sources of healthy feedback. Working within your school's or denomination's requirements for who evaluates you, take time to select people who are "comfortable with providing meaningful evaluation, and who will take the time and care to communicate this evaluation to you."[12]

Feedback from nonprofessional (lay) leaders and members who serve on the front lines of ministry alongside you can give you a unique and critical perspective about how they see who you are and what you bring to the ministry setting. This perspective "from the pew" is one that even the most qualified clergy member or faculty member cannot offer.[13]

The more people you have speaking truth into your life, the better. You will need to consult your school's specific requirements as to the number of evaluators needed during your internship. Although each school has a different process, understand that the feedback you receive from this circle of friends will be one of the greatest highlights of your internship—if you take advantage of the feedback given to you.

Learning through Theological Reflection

At the end of all internships at Dallas Theological Seminary, each student comes into our offices for a one-on-one meeting with me or with a member of my staff. One of the questions we ask every intern is, "What did God teach you during this season of life?" With that one simple question, the stories of reflection are fascinating. This time during the exit interviews is absolutely the highlight of my semester.

We hear stories about students rediscovering the faithfulness of God, even when they themselves have not been faithful. We hear stories about students learning humility as they come face-to-face with their own inadequacies in meeting the physical needs, such as medical care, money, home and shelter, and food, and the spiritual needs of the people they serve at their internship sites. We hear stories about students realizing how dry their spiritual lives have become, seeing the Bible as merely a textbook and not a source of life. We hear stories about students uncovering a sense of God's leading that they have not noticed for years. We hear students making their faith their own. All of these students are reflecting theologically.

In the discipline of field education, the process of reflecting theologically goes by many names—theological reflection, experiential theology, pastoral theology, functional theology, and the theological interpretation of experience. Your school probably has a particular term or a particular model that faculty will introduce to you in helping you reflect biblically, theologically, historically, and culturally. Sometimes these models are introduced in either an introduction to theology class or a field education seminar. No matter the title of the process, reflecting as a Christian helps you link your current human and social reality with the timeless truths of God. Theological reflection helps to reveal the intersection between your story and the biblical story.[14]

Theology Permeates Ministry

All of our relational spheres in life have theological significance as places of service to God and to our neighbor. Vocational service also reflects theology. The question every student—and every Christian, for that matter—must continually ask is how does his or her theology affect how he or she does ministry in the context where he or she serves? While you can operate at an idealistic level in the isolation of theory, in reality your actions reveal your theology and your assumptions.

We are all theologians. This theologizing happens at both the conscious and the unconscious level on a daily basis. Any time you ask questions such as, "Where is God in this?" or "What does God want me to learn from this?" you are participating in theological reflection. Any time you wonder about God, your faith, your beliefs, or your values, you are taking part in theological reflection. In theological reflection in the ministry context, the classroom and the real world meet. This is the heart of the internship.

The big questions asked in theological reflection are, "What do the theological sources of your faith say about your experience?" and "What is your experience teaching you about God, yourself, your theology, your assumptions, and your ministry to others?" Theological reflection is asking about the meaning behind the activity and interpreting this meaning from the perspective of faith in the Christian message. In theological reflection you integrate your theology training with your ministry setting, allowing your faith to influence your personal, social, and ministry life.

Having some disconnect between our formal theology (what we say we believe) and our functional theology (how we actually live) is not uncommon.[15] When you reflect theologically on your actions, the disconnect between what you say you believe and how you really live comes to light. In testing your beliefs, you may discover that things you assumed were true are not. At that point, you have to decide either to continue to live with this incongruence or to seek a solution. The exciting thing is that in the process of theological reflection, your faith can grow stronger as you seek to live out revealed truth in your daily life. Through theological reflection, you have a greater sense of God's presence in your life and a chance to discover how your faith meshes with your daily life.[16]

Theological reflection provides the means needed to discern life and ministry decisions. Through theological reflection, you are no longer a child, as the apostle Paul puts it, "tossed to and fro by the waves and carried about by every wind of doctrine, by human cunning, by craftiness in deceitful schemes" (Eph. 4:14). Instead of allowing the latest fad, the dominant culture, or your own mixed motives to guide your life and ministry decisions, theological reflection allows you to operate with a "theological template that sorts and organizes the data of life" on the singular Christian message of God.[17]

Your Mentor's Role in Theological Reflection

Theological reflection is a dynamic relationship that is both an art and a science. Your mentor's role is to make sure this conversation takes place. He or she cannot force you to reflect and to make changes. Rather, your mentor creates the environment where change becomes desirable and where the Holy Spirit can work (John 14:16-17; John 16:13-14). Ultimately, the presence of the Holy Spirit is what enables you to move beyond cognitive recognition of the need for change to actual obedience.

Your mentor seeks to assist you in seeing God at work in the normality of daily life. This is why it is important to have a mentor who is theologically grounded and who is perceptive in the workings of God in both your life and in the ministry setting where you are working. Both you and your mentor must be intentional, making sure theological reflection takes place. If your mentor does not schedule time for theological reflection, it probably will not happen due to the busyness of the ministry schedule.

Some schools also use peer-led reflection in small groups on campus as a platform for this discussion. These groups may meet before the start of the internship, during the course of the internship, or after the completion of the internship. For example, on our campus, students are placed into peer-led spiritual formation groups for their first two years where they can wrestle with theological reflection in a safe environment. Check with your school to find out if a small-group reflection component is one of the internship requirements.

If your school requires a formal exit interview at the conclusion of your internship, part of this interview may also include theological reflection. Your school may require you to write a paper, theologically reflecting on your experiences during the internship. Again, check with your school to find out the specific requirements.

Steps in Theological Reflection

The best way for me to discuss theological reflection with you is to work through an example. Suppose you are responsible for a young adults Bible study at your internship site. During your entire internship, you have invested much time and emotional energy into making this Bible study a success. One night, while checking your e-mails, you receive an e-mail from a young woman who has been attending the Bible study for the last three months. For sake of the illustration, let's call her "Sue." While not a core member of the study group, Sue has been coming faithfully and has seemed to enjoy both the Bible study and the fellowship. You have had a couple of great conversations with her after the meetings, and she seems to have connected with several of the other women in the group.

In her e-mail, Sue informs you that she will no longer be coming to the Bible study. She says that life has gotten really busy for her recently and that she is overcommitted. She expresses her appreciation for the hard work you have put into the study and is very gracious in her e-mail. Nevertheless, you feel frustrated and hurt by her e-mail. You end up staying up later than normal rehashing the e-mail and your conversations with her and second-guessing your own actions. You even begin to question your effectiveness with the Bible study in the first place.

At your next mentor meeting, your mentor asks how the young adults Bible study is going. Once again, you feel the frustration from this e-mail and share your frustrations with your mentor. Although you know that you should not let this one e-mail bother you, it does and your mentor can see the frustration in your face.

In moving the conversation to productive theological reflection, your mentor might take you through the following steps.

STEP 1: DESCRIBE THE EVENT

The first step in theological reflection is to identify and describe a significant ministry experience for analysis and reflection. This e-mail event is the situation we are using to illustrate each of the steps that follow. But maybe your situation is not a frustrating e-mail. Maybe your situation is a conflict that you had with a co-worker. Maybe your situation is a challenging conversation you had to have with a church member. Maybe your situation was a difficult hospital visitation or the death of a close friend.

One clue to identifying incidents for fruitful theological reflection is to notice encounters from your everyday life. Strong feelings generated by remembering an event are a sign that you may be hearing God speak to you. Look for those situations where you were called on to stretch or to develop new learning or where you struggled or experienced pain. Challenges

(novelty, difficult goals, conflict, and hardship) are critical opportunities to learn to do theology in the context of ministry
because embedded theology is active.[18]

With this situation or event in your mind, play the role of a
good investigative reporter in describing the scene in as much
detail as possible. Give a detailed, factual, specific, and concrete
description of what took place.[19] Use the following questions as
a springboard for this discussion:

1. What happened?
2. Who was involved? Identify the persons involved in the
   incident—ages, gender, race, vocation, socioeconomic
   level, marital status, relationships.
3. What was your role in the situation?
4. How did you respond in the situation? What did you
   do or say?
5. How did the other people respond to you?
6. How did the situation end?

At this stage, no detail is too minute. So in describing Sue's
e-mail incident, you would tell your mentor about all of the
objective facts surrounding the situation: details about the Bible
study, details about the participants, details about Sue, details
about the e-mail.

STEP 2: IDENTIFY YOUR EMOTIONS
Now that you have the facts on the table, the next step is to talk
about the emotions you felt during the situation. In the e-mail
example, you describe the facts of the incident but you also
identify the emotions you felt. In this case, you felt hurt and
frustrated. Upon further reflection, you relate these feelings
to the sense that your worth as a Bible study leader has been
questioned by someone. Wanting to be liked by everyone, you

are hurt because this one person is no longer coming to your Bible study. While you know cognitively that this is an irrational thought, the emotion you feel is strong.

A mark of an emotionally healthy individual is emotional self-awareness. Emotional self-awareness is ability to both recognize a feeling as it is happening and to be able to name that feeling. In our lives, we experience dozens of emotions, along with combinations, variations, mutations, and subtleties. Researchers in the field of emotional intelligence usually discuss emotion "families," including anger, sadness, fear, enjoyment, love, surprise, disgust, and shame.[20] Taking the time to name your emotions in a situation helps sort out what is going on internally as you reflect on a specific event. A simple way to think about this is completing the statement, "I felt _____ when _____ because _____."[21]

Here are some other questions to jumpstart the discussion.

1. How did you feel when this situation happened? Were you anxious or excited about it? Sad? Energized? Upset? Why?
2. What challenged, stimulated, or disturbed you?
3. What bodily sensations did you experience? Upset stomach? Sleeplessness?
4. What was happening to others in the situation?
5. How did you respond? What did you do? What did you say? Why?

All emotions are important in theologically reflecting on a situation. Remember that you are both a cognitive and an affective individual. Many times your emotional and spontaneous responses to life may help identify areas where you are wrestling with God and where you are searching for meaning.[22] So, returning to the e-mail situation, naming the frustration you felt upon receiving a seemingly harmless e-mail and talking about why you felt that frustration are important. As you reflect on that night and the e-mail, you begin to discuss with your mentor how you felt.

STEP 3: LISTEN TO THE RESOURCES

When you take time to think about the big questions of life, you will notice no lack of media and people telling you what to believe. Television, radio, movies, newspapers, billboards, Web sites, family members, friends, classmates, pastors, professors, and culture bombard you with information to consider. The question then becomes what information is relevant. As a person who wants to reflect theologically, where should you turn and to whom should you listen?

With so much information telling you what to think and do, a matrix can help you organize these various resources in a way that can uncover meaning useful to you. What author Abigail Johnson calls a "clear and deliberate process" can help you think through the experiences of life through the lens of faith.[23] Theological reflection brings to bear in the discussion the various resources available to a Christian. These resources include the following:

- The biblical message
- Christian heritage
- Cultural expressions
- Personal experience

Let me briefly describe each of these. In theological reflection, you have a choice as to your starting point. One option is to have what is called an "anthropological" starting point. With this starting point, you first look at the experiences of life, then try to understand the meaning of God's message to the world. The other option is to have a "revelatory" starting point. With this starting point, you look first at the revealed message of God

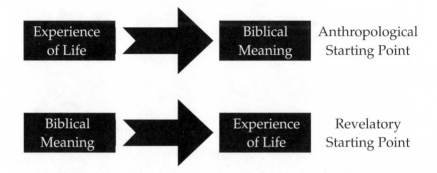

Figure 5.1. Starting Points of Theological Reflection

in Scripture and church tradition, then move to explore human implications.[24]

Biblical Message

I believe very strongly that foundational to any discussion of theological reflection from a Christian perspective is the role the biblical message plays. Theologians Stan Grenz and Roger Olson stress that the Bible provides the "foundation for our lives as Christians. It is both the source for understanding ourselves as God's people and the norm that informs us as to what we should believe and how we should live. The Bible therefore is indispensable to theology. Whatever else it may be, our theology had better be biblical."[25]

When faced with a decision or when trying to reconcile your actions, the first place to look is a scriptural foundation. Consider these questions:

1. What specific biblical passage addresses the experience you are facing?
2. What insights or solutions can you find in the Bible addressing this particular situation?

3. What biblical person or model can be used in this situation?
4. What theological issues or themes were present? Sin? Grace? Mercy? Faith? Hope? Love? Prayer? Suffering? Christ?

Not all theology is equal and not all theology is in the vein of historical, orthodox Christian theology. Christian theologians in every age have acknowledged the biblical writings as a norm for Christian theology.[26] As a believer in Christ, my approach to theology cannot be detached from the biblical text and two millenniums of Christian orthodoxy.

So, maybe in reflecting on the e-mail incident with Sue, you relate your feelings to the prophet Jeremiah who also knew the frustration of ministry firsthand. Perhaps you are drawn to a psalm that talks about feeling betrayed. Or possibly you are drawn to the Pauline letters or the Gospels, which talk about servanthood in leadership.

Christian Heritage
One shortfall of many churches in the United States today is that they have no sense of history. I grew up in a church and a denominational setting with no real sense of historical perspective, of Christian heritage. I was never introduced to the great men and women of faith from the church of old. I was never exposed to the creeds of the faith. I was never shown how orthodoxy was defended against the heresies of its day. How shallow our perspective if we think we are the only believers or the only generation to wrestle with a particular theological question.

The writer of Ecclesiastes knew this very well: "What has been is what will be, and what has been done is what will be done, and there is nothing new under the sun. Is there a thing of which it is said, 'See, this is new'? It has been already in the ages before us. There is no remembrance of former things, nor will there be any remembrance of later things yet to be among those who come after" (Eccles. 1:9-11).

Our rich Christian tradition includes both insights from the biblical message and the experiences and wisdom of historical Christian orthodoxy throughout the centuries. Grenz and Olson note,

> Our heritage is a reference point in that it contains examples of previous attempts to fulfill the theological mandate from which we today can learn. Looking at the past alerts us to some of the pitfalls we should avoid, some of the land mines that could trip us up, and some of the cul-de-sacs or blind alleys that are not worth our exploration. . . . The purpose of using the tool of heritage is to connect us with the church of all ages as we seek to construct an orthodox Christian theology in the contemporary situation.[27]

Drawing on Scripture and church tradition helps to keep you grounded against the pull of the latest theologies of culture. Instead, we are grounded in the faith of those who have walked before us. Here are some questions to consider:

1. How have other Christians in history dealt with the same issue you are experiencing?
2. What insights or solutions can you find in church history addressing this particular situation?

So, while e-mail is a modern invention, the saints of old knew very well what it was like to pour oneself into a ministry and to have someone not respond favorably. The church fathers talked about having a humble spirit in service, reminding you that ministry is about God's glory and not your glory. Church history teaches you that having numbers in a Bible study does not signify value in ministry.

Cultural Experience

While I caution against elevating culture to being equivalent with the biblical message or with church heritage, still remember that we do not live in a cultural vacuum. The biblical message must be the foundation and the heritage of the church also must be consulted, but you must also become a student of culture by examining the role of cultural experience. In theological reflection, you put your own experiences, both personal and cultural, into a "genuine conversation" with the norm of religious heritage from the biblical message and Christian tradition.[28]

In their foundational book on theological reflection, *Method in Ministry: Theological Reflection and Christian Ministry*, James Whitehead and Evelyn Eaton Whitehead define culture as the "formative symbols and ongoing interpretations that shape our world-view, as well as the social roles and political structures

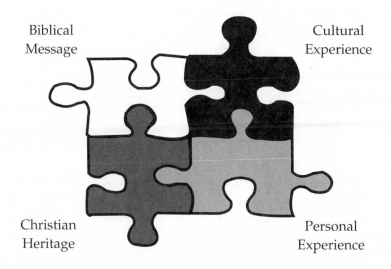

Biblical
Message

Cultural
Experience

Christian
Heritage

Personal
Experience

Figure 5.2. Theological Conversation between Religious Heritage and Experience

that shape social life."[29] Culture is an understanding of how your particular heritage and setting have developed your convictions, values, beliefs, and biases.

On the broadest level, culture involves the historical time period and geographical location in which you live. Culture may include religion (Christian, religious, nonreligious, pluralistic), ethnic environment (homogeneous, multicultural, minority in majority culture), political and economic environment (democracy, socialism, conservative, liberal), media (sources of news and entertainment; exposure to radio, TV, and printed materials), traditions (holidays, historical events, dietary habits, fashion), and art (purpose, emphasis on freedom of expression).[30] The local community where you were born and raised has its unique and particular combination of these elements that constitute its culture.

Along with personal experiences, which I talk about later in this chapter, culture plays a significant role in teaching you how to relate to people and how to fulfill roles. As Whitehead and Whitehead note, "Reality does not exist as 'raw data' that all human beings interpret the same way. Instead, human experience always comes 'cooked'—seasoned in the communal pot, part of a cultural stew of expectations and prohibitions, of significance and symbol, that prevail in any group. We know the world only in culturally-formed ways."[31]

Just as a fish is unaware of the water it swims in, you are usually unaware of the cultural influences that affect your behavior. According to Lynne Delay and Maxine Dalton, cultural researchers with the Center for Creative Leadership, culture usually functions through what we perceive as "common sense understanding of reality" (this is how the world is) and "widely accepted expectations of appropriate behavior" (this is how you act around here). Theological reflection helps you discover your cultural assumptions. Delay and Dalton stress, "Such critical examination can be disconcerting, leaving us with a sense that our world is out of focus. Examining our culture's assumptions calls into question the worldview that makes sense to us, the perspective through which we make sense to us, the perspective through which we make sense of our own lives."[32]

Personal Experience
Just as you do not minister in a cultural vacuum, you also do not minister in a personal vacuum. Remember that you bring your own history to the internship setting. When you are faced with a particular situation, many times you may have faced a similar situation before. Ask yourself how you dealt with this situation in the past.

According to Whitehead and Whitehead, personal experience is "that set of ideas, feelings, biases, and insights which a particular minister and community bring to a pastoral reflection. Experience thus embraces not only ideas or 'understandings' but a wide range of rational and extra-rational convictions, hopes, and apprehensions."[33] Our personal heritage or experiences have made us who we are today. So, exploring your life story and how you have dealt with similar situations before is important.

Part of your personal experience comes from your family's culture. Family culture is the blueprint of actions and values you learned because of the way your family related and lived out roles. This culture is the one that influences most people to the greatest degree, for good or for bad. This environment is the one in which most people, until they reach their late thirties and early forties, have spent the most time. Families develop certain patterns of thinking and behavior.[34]

Still another level of personal experience can be seen in various subcultures. These are an assortment of environments outside the family culture but distinct from mainstream culture. Examples of these can be social organizations, church traditions, or parachurch settings. For people who strongly identify with a particular subculture, its effect on their heritage may be great.[35]

Just as examining your culture provides an understanding of how your particular heritage and setting have developed your convictions, values, beliefs, and biases, your personal experiences also contribute to your development over time. Consider these questions:

1. Have you faced similar situations in your past? If so, how did you deal with that situation?
2. Growing up, how were you taught to respond in such situations?
3. What have you learned from your past experiences about how to deal with conflict?
4. What leadership styles have you learned through your personal experiences?
5. What communication styles have you learned through your personal experiences?
6. What biases have you developed over time through your personal experiences?

As you reflect on Sue's e-mail and your response, maybe you remember that you dealt with a similar situation in the past where a person questioned your leadership. Perhaps you grew up in a family that did not give approval to you, so you find yourself seeking approval from other people, including Sue. Possibly you have learned through the years to take any rejection personally. Maybe your automatic reaction to criticism is to be defensive.

STEP 4: APPLICATION

The final step in theological reflection, application, is the most important. Theological reflection is ultimately a call to application in your life. Unless you move past the intellectual exercise of theological reflection to action, then all of the previous steps are really done in vain.[36] Understanding yourself is simply a means to the end of practicing theological truth in your day-to-day life.[37]

The New Testament letter of James speaks of the foolishness of reflection without application: "But don't just listen to God's word. You must do what it says. Otherwise, you are only fooling yourselves. For if you listen to the word and don't obey, it is like glancing at your face in a mirror. You see yourself, walk away, and forget what you look like. But if you look carefully into the perfect law that sets you free, and if you do what it says and don't forget what you heard, then God will bless you for doing it" (James 1:22-25 NLT).

So, in working through theological reflection toward application, discuss the following questions:

1. What questions still linger from the situation? What feelings remain raw or unprocessed? What thoughts still seem unsettled?
2. Were you challenged to change present actions or beliefs? What may you do differently in the future? Has your reflection opened up new possibilities?
3. What have you learned about yourself from this experience and your reflection?
4. What have you learned about other people from this experience and your reflection?
5. What have you learned about God from this experience and your reflection?
6. How do you need to trust God to work in this situation? What about in future situations?
7. What are the implications for yourself as a minister? What skills have you learned here? What are your weaknesses? What are your strengths?
8. What will you do now? What is your next step?

As we conclude the illustration of Sue's e-mail, what did you learn? Maybe you learned that you were basing your own identity as a minister or as a person on the approval of others. As a result of this insight, you begin to work on basing your identity on your connection with the Godhead instead. Perhaps you learned to invest in the lives of people but to leave the results to the Holy Spirit instead of your own efforts. Possibly you learned that you have a past of reacting to similar situations in frustration, and you begin to work with your mentor and others to learn more productive response techniques. One simple e-mail may contain great learning possibilities if you allow yourself the opportunity to reflect theologically.

Are You Ready to Learn?

The payoff for an internship is your personal and spiritual growth. By being open to the feedback of others and by taking the time to reflect theologically, you have the opportunity to receive the wonderful gift of growth. And it truly is a gift. In my own life, the times of greatest growth have happened when I listened to the loving critique of a friend and when I took time to ask the big questions of faith. Make sure you slow down long enough to allow God to speak to you.

Development is a process. Moving along the path to becoming more Christlike or becoming a better leader does not proceed quickly. One does not instantly become a godly leader once the diploma is in hand. Leadership development in the context of ministry is a lifelong journey that also requires both human effort and God's empowerment, just as with spiritual growth.

Taking a leadership class, reading the latest leadership book, having a great six-month internship, attending a weekend leadership conference, or even attending the right school does not make a person a leader. However, those good things, along with many other life experiences, can create an environ-ment where the Holy Spirit can transform you over time into the godly servant leader God desires. Much of leadership is developed as you allow God's Spirit to work through the people who surround you, your life experiences, your education, and God's Holy Word to transform you into a person in the likeness of Christ and into a godly servant leader.

Questions for Reflection

1. When was a time when you honestly benefited from the feedback of another person? Was it a teacher? A coach? A parent? A pastor? A friend? Why were his or her words beneficial?

2. Have you ever received feedback that was not benefi-cial? What is the difference between beneficial and not beneficial feedback in your life?

3. In your internship site, whom do you need to receive feedback from?

4. Do you feel like you are aware of your own emotions in a given situation? What examples can you think of to support your conclusion?

5. How have the following been influenced by your cul-tural experience and personal experience?

Interpersonal communication
Household management
Expression of affection
Conflict management
Time management
Money management
Views of competition and ambition
Significance of family and personal reputation

Acceptable vocational goals
View of other cultures and ethnic groups

6. Based on your cultural and personal experiences, how
    have you learned to deal with challenging situations?
    Are your reactions theologically sound?
7. As you reflect on this season of your life (school, in-
    ternship, and relationships), what big lesson have you
    learned about God? What big lesson have you learned
    about yourself?

EPILOGUE
Playing in the Dirt

THE GOAL OF *MINISTRY GREENHOUSE* IS TO HELP YOU explore the components necessary for beneficial leadership development through internship. My prayer is that you will be placed in a learning environment where the Holy Spirit will use you as an instrument of transformation in the lives of other people. But, more important, my prayer is that you will be placed in a learning environment where the Holy Spirit will transform you to be more like Jesus Christ.

One of the lessons of life that I learned early in ministry is that ministry with people is messy work. Pastors sometimes joke and say, "I would love the ministry if it were not for the people," but ministry *is* a people business. The messiness of ministry does come from other people disappointing you, failing you, discouraging you, frustrating you, and even attacking you. Some of the greatest joys and the greatest frustrations in my life have come in ministering to and through people in my church. Let no one try to convince you that ministry is always rosy, because there are days when ministry is anything but rose smelling.

Yet, true personal growth takes place in the midst of ministry's messiness. In the trials of working with other people, I have discovered my greatest liabilities and have grown the most. In the midst of the messiness of ministry, I have been able to connect "head knowledge" from books and classes with the "heart knowledge" of true ownership of what I believe. In the midst of trials, I was able to claim my own faith expression—not my youth minister's, not my parents', but mine. Life's best lessons are learned when we come "into firsthand relationship with human beings suffering from the maladies that afflict mankind."[1] This transformation does not happen overnight. Experience takes time.

Therefore, the best environment for your internship is one that fully engages you in the messiness of ministry. Learning takes place as you deal with the tension or disequilibrium between your perceptions and your reality, causing you to consider the validity of your skills, values, and approaches. Learning takes place when these challenges force you to reconcile the differences and when you have to evaluate your old ways of thinking. What an internship can do is serve as the gym where ministerial and spiritual muscles are built. You will only develop when you are challenged. And this challenge includes people.

Marketplace theologian R. Paul Stevens puts it this way: "If God has come in the flesh, and if God keeps coming to us in our fleshy existence, then all of life is shot through with meaning. Earth is crammed with heaven, and heaven (when we finally get there) will be crammed with earth. Nothing wasted. Nothing lost. Nothing secular. Nothing absurd. . . . All are grist for the mill of a down-to-earth spirituality."[2]

The purpose of your college or seminary is not to force you to grow mentally, emotionally, physically, and spiritually. Rather, its purpose is to create a learning environment where you have a greater likelihood of success. Nevertheless, you have to choose to plant yourself inside that greenhouse. An internship is one of the best possible learning environments in which you can place yourself. Plant yourself, and watch God grow you.

To this end we always pray for you, that our God may make you worthy of his calling and may fulfill every resolve for good and every work of faith by his power, so that the name of our Lord Jesus may be glorified in you, and you in him, according to the grace of our God and the Lord Jesus Christ.

—2 Thessalonians 1:11-12

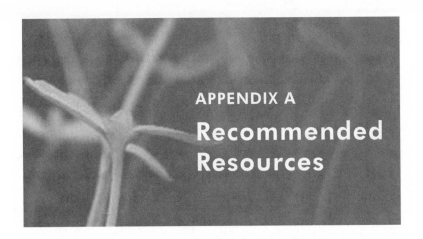

APPENDIX A

Recommended Resources

WHAT FOLLOWS IS A LIST OF THE RESOURCES I HAVE found most helpful as a coordinator of seminary internships. While this book contains a bibliography, I want to also recommend resources so that you can read the best of the current books available on the subject of internships. This list includes a mix of resources that target both the religious community and the business community.

Anderson, Keith R., and Randy D. Reese. *Spiritual Mentoring: A Guide for Seeking and Giving Direction.* Downers Grove, IL: InterVarsity Press, 1999.

Biehl, Bobb. *Mentoring: Confidence in Finding a Mentor and Becoming One.* Nashville: Broadman and Holman, 1996.

Donovan, Craig P., and Jim Garnett. *Internships for Dummies.* New York: Hungry Minds, 2001.

Hendricks, Howard G. *Developing Leadership through Mentoring and Coaching.* DVD. Dallas, TX: Center for Christian Leadership at Dallas Theological Seminary, 2003.

Hendricks, Howard G., and William Hendricks. *As Iron Sharpens Iron: Building Character in a Mentoring Relationship.* Chicago: Moody Press, 1995.

McCauley, Cynthia and Ellen Van Velsor, eds. *The Center for Creative Leadership Handbook of Leadership Development*. 2nd ed. San Francisco: Jossey-Bass, 2004.

Miller, Arthur F. Jr., and William Hendricks. *The Power of Uniqueness: How to Become Who You Really Are*. Grand Rapids, MI: Zondervan, 1999.

Pyle, William T., and Mary Alice Seals, eds. *Experiencing Ministry Supervision: A Field-Based Approach*. Nashville: Broadman and Holman, 1995.

Smith, Gordon T. *Courage and Calling: Embracing Your God-Given Potential*. Downers Grove, IL: InterVarsity Press, 1999.

Zachary, Lois J. *The Mentor's Guide: Facilitating Effective Learning Relationships*. San Francisco: Jossey-Bass, 2000.

APPENDIX B

General Ministry Leadership Competencies

THIS LIST INCLUDES GENERAL MINISTRY COMPETENCIES that are applicable to all leaders in all ministry settings. Much of this list comes from the latest research in transformational leadership and emotional intelligence. For each item, assess yourself on a 1 to 5 scale (1 meaning strongly disagree and 5 meaning strongly agree).

Communication	I am able to communicate effectively with others both verbally and in writing.	1 2 3 4 5
Conflict management	I am able to engage all parties, understand the differing perspectives, and find a common solution.	1 2 3 4 5
Decision making	I am able to consider all of the consequences of a decision and make that decision easily.	1 2 3 4 5
Developing others	I am able to cultivate people's abilities and to offer timely and constructive feedback.	1 2 3 4 5
Emotional self-awareness	I am aware of my emotions and how they affect my performance and myself.	1 2 3 4 5

Empathy	I am able to identify and understand another person's feelings or point of view.	1 2 3 4 5
Encouragement	I am able to offer encouragement to others in appropriate ways.	1 2 3 4 5
Flexibility	I am flexible in dealing with my life and the lives of others around me. I can juggle multiple demands.	1 2 3 4 5
Initiative	I participate in challenging opportunities to change, grow, and improve.	1 2 3 4 5
Listening	I am able to listen to others with my ears, eyes, and heart.	1 2 3 4 5
Pastoral care	I am able to provide care for others in a variety of contexts (for example, crisis, hospital, grief, marriage).	1 2 3 4 5
Personal faith commitment	I have an active and dynamic faith. I am able to share my faith in appropriate ways.	1 2 3 4 5
Personal integrity	I am a person of my word. I live a consistent principle-centered life.	1 2 3 4 5
Planning and organizing	I am able to plan, prioritize, and implement my plans easily.	1 2 3 4 5
Risk taking	I am willing to take risks and learn from the accompanying mistakes.	1 2 3 4 5
Self-care	I am taking care of myself physically and emotionally.	1 2 3 4 5
Self-control	I am able to exercise appropriate control of my emotions, my use of time, and my money.	1 2 3 4 5
Serving	I am able to see the needs of others and willing to serve others sacrificially.	1 2 3 4 5

Spiritual discipline	I have an active devotional life that includes Scripture reading, prayer, and meditation.	1 2 3 4 5
Stress management	I am able to react to stress positively and work well under pressure.	1 2 3 4 5
Teamwork and collaboration	I am able to work well with others with respect, helpfulness, and cooperation.	1 2 3 4 5
Transparency	I relate to others in an authentic way and am open to sharing myself with others in appropriate ways.	1 2 3 4 5
Trustworthiness	I am dependable and can be trusted to carry out responsibilities without constant supervision.	1 2 3 4 5
Visioning	I am able to enlist others in the organization to work toward a common vision.	1 2 3 4 5

Specific Ministry Skill Competencies

Understanding Ministry Contexts

___ I have worked with children.

___ I have worked with junior-high or high-school youth.

___ I have worked with college-age or young adults.

___ I have worked with married couples.

___ I have worked with single adults.

___ I have worked with parents, single and married.

___ I have worked with senior adults.

___ I have worked with people of another culture.

___ I have worked in a rural setting.

___ I have worked in an urban setting.

___ I have worked in a suburban setting.

___ I have worked in a small-sized church or ministry organization.

___ I have worked in a middle-sized church or ministry organization.

___ I have worked in a large-sized church or ministry organization.

___ I have worked with male coworkers.

___ I have worked with female coworkers.

Other: _____

Ministry Leadership

___ I have supported the development of a mission or vision statement for a ministry.

___ I have supported the development of a strategy for a ministry.

___ I have facilitated a small group.

___ I have trained teachers, small group leaders, or other ministry leaders.

___ I have trained leadership teams.

___ I have directed a children's program or event.

___ I have directed a youth program or event.

___ I have directed an adult program or event.

___ I have directed a camp or retreat.

___ I have participated in starting or planting a church.

Other: _____

Administration

___ I have developed and managed a budget.

___ I have directed a fund-raising or stewardship program.

___ I have delegated responsibilities to others.

___ I have worked with other staff members.

___ I have worked with an elder board, deacon board, or governing board.

___ I have attended a local denominational meeting.

___ I have attended a regional or national denominational meeting.

___ I have served on a congregational committee or ministry team.

___ I have led a congregational committee or ministry team.

____ I have planned a community-wide event.
____ I have produced publicity for an event or a ministry.
____ I have an understanding of facilities management.
____ I have worked with an administrative assistant.
____ I have developed good time-management skills.

Other: _____

Teaching

____ I have selected teaching curriculum.
____ I have written teaching curriculum.
____ I have taught in a small-group context.
____ I have taught in a large-group context.
____ I have used different teaching methodologies (for example, lecture, discussion, interactive).
____ I have developed and used audiovisual materials in my teaching (for example, PowerPoint, videos).

Other: _____

Evangelism and Discipleship

____ I have preached an evangelistic sermon.
____ I have taught an evangelistic Bible study.
____ I have presented the gospel within a relationship.
____ I have presented the gospel to a stranger.
____ I have taught a new members' or new believers' class.
____ I have mentored a believer in a one-on-one context.
____ I have taught evangelism training.
____ I have directed a visitation or an evangelism ministry.
____ I have planned a community-wide event.

___ I have developed a discipleship program.
___ I have directed or developed a hospitality ministry.

Other: _____

Corporate Worship Leadership

___ I have made announcements in corporate worship.
___ I have led prayer in corporate worship.
___ I have led music in corporate worship.
___ I have preached or taught in corporate worship.
___ I have served as an assisting minister or a liturgist in corporate worship.
___ I have developed a sermon series.
___ I have learned to work with the church calendar and lectionary.
___ I have led or presided over communion in corporate worship.
___ I have planned and conducted a baptismal service.
___ I have preached a children's sermon.
___ I have worked with a ministry team in planning corporate worship.

Other: _____

Cross-Cultural Ministry

___ I have friendships with people of another culture.
___ I have participated in a local cross-cultural ministry.
___ I have directed a local cross-cultural ministry.
___ I have participated in a cross-cultural mission trip.

___ I have led a cross-cultural mission trip.
___ I have traveled outside my own country.
___ I have researched a people group.
___ I have taught or preached in a cross-cultural context.
___ I have shared the gospel in a cross-cultural context.
___ I have taught an English-as-a-second-language class.

Other: _____

Pastoral Care and Counseling

___ I am a good listener.
___ I am good at asking questions.
___ I have counseled on marital issues or divorce.
___ I have counseled on parenting issues.
___ I have counseled on ethical issues.
___ I have counseled on sexual issues.
___ I have counseled on doctrinal or spiritual issues.
___ I have counseled on emotional or mental issues.
___ I have counseled on health issues.
___ I have conducted premarital counseling.
___ I have conducted a wedding.
___ I have counseled bereaved family members.
___ I have conducted a funeral or a graveside service.
___ I have visited a person in the hospital.
___ I have visited a person in prison or jail.
___ I have visited a person in a retirement home.
___ I have facilitated a support group.
___ I am familiar with pastoral care resources (for example,
     agencies, books, Web sites, counselors).

Other: _____

Academic Teaching and Research

___ I have taught in an academic classroom setting.
___ I have facilitated classroom discussion groups.
___ I have developed a syllabus for a class.
___ I have developed a bibliography for a class.
___ I have developed and used thorough lesson plans.
___ I have designed and graded assignments and papers.
___ I have tutored students.
___ I have attended departmental or faculty meetings.
___ I have attended academic professional conferences.

Other: _____

Media Arts and Communications

___ I have written a book, magazine article, or journal article for publication.
___ I have written a stage play, teleplay, or screenplay.
___ I have sung or played an instrument before an audience.
___ I have conducted a band or an orchestra.
___ I have composed or arranged music.
___ I have danced before an audience.
___ I have acted before an audience.
___ I have been involved in aspects of drama production.
___ I have been involved in aspects of film or video production.
___ I have been involved in aspects of audio production.
___ I paint or sculpt.
___ I design with textile arts.
___ I design computer graphics.
___ I design Web sites.

___ I have written a blog.
___ I have created podcasts.
___ I have created Web videocasts.
___ I have used PowerPoint in a presentation.
___ I have used film or video clips in worship or education.

Other: _____

APPENDIX D

Sample Goals

Sample Goal	Sample Goal Strategy	Sample Goal Measurement
1. To deepen my personal worship time in my devotion to God	Establish a consistent time each day for personal devotion (prayer and Bible study).	Have a consistent personal devotion time of thirty uninterrupted minutes at least four days a week.
	Focus my personal devotional reading time on the attributes of God, focusing on the Psalms in particular.	Memorize one verse per month that focuses on the attributes of God and say it from memory to one person a week
	Increase Scripture memorization, focusing on verses that reveal God's character and attributes.	Ask my ministry mentor to hold me accountable to my personal devotional time on a weekly basis.
	Read John Ortberg's *The Life You've Always Wanted*	Read *The Life You've Always Wanted* by January 1 and discuss the insights from that book with my ministry mentor.

Sample Goal	Sample Goal Strategy	Sample Goal Measurement
2. To show more tangible signs of love to my spouse	Discover my spouse's "love language" to show tangible signs of love.	By May, spend an entire evening with my spouse to discuss my spouse's "love language" and ways to show tangible signs of love.
	Become more intentional in praying with my spouse and praying for my spouse.	Have a consistent prayer time of at least ten uninterrupted minutes with my spouse at least four days a week.
	Spend more quality time with my spouse on a weekly basis	Have a weekly "date night" with just my spouse on Friday nights.
	Attend a marriage retreat with my spouse.	Attend our church's marriage retreat with my spouse in February of this year.
3. To develop patience in my relationships	Discuss with my ministry mentor situations in which I find it hard to be patient, and create a plan of development and accountability.	Include discussions on patience in my weekly meetings with my ministry mentor.
	Seek input from my family and those under my leadership about my impatient behavior.	On a weekly basis, ask those under my leadership to hold me accountable in my development of patience.
	Expose myself to Scripture that deals directly with patience.	By June, memorize three verses that deal with the area of patience.

Sample Goal	Sample Goal Strategy	Sample Goal Measurement
4. To be more consistent in my own devotional study of God's Word	Purchase a One Year Bible and begin using it as my devotional Bible during this internship.	Purchase a One Year Bible by August and begin using it in my daily devotion time.
	Ask my ministry mentor to hold me accountable by asking me what I have learned in my devotion time.	Have my ministry mentor ask me every week about what I am learning in my devotion time.
5. To deal with my anger in a productive, God-honoring way	Learn to recognize situations in which I find anger controlling me.	Ask my ministry mentor to hold me accountable for my anger.
	Discuss with my ministry mentor those situations in which I find anger controlling me, and develop a plan of improvement and accountability.	Complete a Scripture study on anger by November 1 and discuss the insights from that book with my ministry mentor.
	Expose myself to scriptures that deal directly with anger.	Read *Make Anger Your Ally* by Neil Clark Warren by January and discuss the insights from that book with my ministry mentor
6. To learn how to perform a wedding	Discuss weddings with my ministry mentor.	Discuss weddings with my ministry mentor by April.
	Observe my ministry mentor in a prewedding counseling session.	Observe a counseling session by August.

Sample Goal	Sample Goal Strategy	Sample Goal Measurement
	Observe my ministry mentor perform a wedding.	Observe a wedding by October.
7. To learn how to develop both a mission and a vision statement for a church (or parachurch organization)	Discuss with my ministry mentor his or her definition of mission and vision for the organization	By November, discuss my ministry mentor's personal mission and vision statement.
	Collect several mission and vision statements from other churches (or parachurch organizations) to study your similarities and differences.	By April, interview five pastors to learn their church's mission and vision statements and understand the process of how their church arrived at their statements.
	Develop a mission and vision statement for my church setting	Include discussions on mission and vision in my weekly meetings with ministry mentor.
8. To learn about Muslim culture for cross-cultural ministry	Interview a Muslim religious leader.	Interview a Muslim religious leader by January.
	Attend a Muslim religious service.	Attend a Muslim religious service by February.
	Read *Answering Islam* by Norman Geisler and Abdul Saleeb.	Read *Answering Islam* and discuss the insights from that book with my ministry mentor by April.

Sample Goal	Sample Goal Strategy	Sample Goal Measurement
	Participate on a short-term mission trip to an Islamic culture.	Participate on a short-term mission trip to an Islamic culture in July.
9. To learn how to select or develop a Bible study curriculum for junior high students on Sunday mornings	Discuss curriculum development with my ministry mentor.	Include discussions on curriculum in my weekly meetings with ministry mentor.
	Review class notes and meet with the Christian education faculty to discuss curriculum development.	Meet with Christian education faculty by October.
	Meet with the youth pastor at my church to learn how the current curriculum was chosen for junior high students.	Interview my youth pastor by December.
	Investigate what curriculum other youth ministries in the area use.	Research five other youth ministries and their curriculum by March.
10. To learn how a board of elders works in a church	Read *The Unity Factor* by Larry Osborne.	Read *The Unity Factor* and discuss the insights from that book with my ministry mentor by October.
	Attend an elders board meeting at my church each semester.	Attend the elders board meeting in October and February.

Sample Goal	Sample Goal Strategy	Sample Goal Measurement
	Interview the chairperson of the elders board at my church.	Interview the chairperson of the elders board by December.
	Interview the senior pastor on issues related to the elders board.	Interview the senior pastor by March.
11. To develop skills in planning a retreat	Recruit a retreat planning committee.	Have the retreat planning committee in place by October.
	Develop a retreat budget and select a retreat location.	Schedule the retreat for February.
	Enlist a retreat speaker and/or worship leader.	Include discussions on retreat planning in my weekly meetings with my ministry mentor.
	Develop registration and publicity plans.	Ask my ministry mentor to evaluate my retreat planning by March.
12. To learn how to prepare and deliver a sermon	Interview other pastors to discuss their sermon preparation habits.	Schedule three pastoral interviews by April.
	Discuss sermon preparation and delivery with my ministry mentor.	Hand in to my ministry mentor one sermon per month to evaluate.
	Deliver a sermon three times during my internship.	Deliver a sermon three times in my church by May.

Sample Goal	Sample Goal Strategy	Sample Goal Measurement
13. To learn how to work with an administrative assistant	Discuss with my ministry mentor his or her understanding of the role of his or her administrative assistant.	Work in the office every Wednesday from 9 a.m. to 12 noon.
	Work weekly in the office to learn firsthand about faculty expectations and utilization of administrative assistants.	Set up a biweekly time with a different administrative assistant to discuss expectations and suggestions.
	Discuss with departmental administrative assistants ways in which faculty work with them and any suggestions they may have on how to capitalize on their services.	By December, discuss with my ministry mentor his or her understanding of the role of his or her administrative assistant.
14. To learn how to encourage my team	Schedule monthly meetings with the church's youth ministry workers.	Start the monthly workers meeting in September.
	Take each of the youth ministry workers out to lunch for a one-on-one time of encouragement.	By May, take all of the youth leaders out to lunch.
	Plan an end-of-year appreciation dinner for the church's youth ministry workers.	Hold an appreciation dinner in May.
	Discuss encouragement with my ministry mentor.	Discuss encouragement weekly with my ministry mentor.

Sample Goal	Sample Goal Strategy	Sample Goal Measurement
15. To improve my small group facilitation skills	Apply to be a small group leader at my church.	Complete my small group leader application by May.
	Attend all of the small group leader training.	Attend the small group leader training in August.
	Lead a small group.	Attend the weekly small group leader training.
	Discuss small group leadership with my ministry mentor.	Discuss small groups weekly with my ministry mentor.

Notes

Chapter 1, Why Internships?

1. Francis A. Lonsway, *The Graduating Student Question-naire: A Study of Five Years of Use 1996-1997 through 2000-2001* (Pittsburgh: The Association of Theological Schools, 2002), 5-6.

2. *Merriam-Webster's Collegiate Dictionary*, 11th ed., s.v. "Seminary."

Chapter 2, What Is God Calling You to Do?

1. Os Guinness, *The Call: Finding and Fulfilling the Central Purpose of Your Life* (Nashville: W Publishing Group, 1998), vii.

2. Ibid., 3-4, 29.

3. Mark R. Schwehn and Dorothy C. Bass, *Leading Lives That Matter: What We Should Do and Who We Should Be* (Grand Rapids, MI: Eerdmans, 2006), 2.

4. Guinness, 31.

5. Martin Luther, "Sunday After Christmas, Luke 2:33-40," in *The Precious and Sacred Writings of Martin Luther*, ed. John Nicholas Lenker (Minneapolis: Lutherans in All Lands, 1905), 10:282.

6. Gary D. Badcock, *The Way of Life: A Theology of Christian Vocation* (Grand Rapids, MI: Eerdmans, 1998), 10, 112.

7. William C. Placher, ed., *Callings: Twenty Centuries of Christian Wisdom on Vocation* (Grand Rapids, MI: Eerdmans, 2005), 2-3.

8. Arthur F. Miller Jr. and William D. Hendricks, *The Power of Uniqueness: How to Become Who You Really Are* (Grand Rapids, MI: Zondervan, 1999), 11.

9. Parker J. Palmer, *Let Your Life Speak: Listening for the Voice of Vocation* (San Francisco: Jossey-Bass, 2000), 10, 15-16, 47.

10. *Merriam-Webster's Collegiate Dictionary*, 11th ed., s.v. "Hypocrisy."

11. Marcus Buckingham and Donald O. Clifton, *Now, Discover Your Strengths* (New York: The Free Press, 2001), 75.

12. Ibid., 67-75.

13. Miller and Hendricks, *Power of Uniqueness*.

14. John Bradley and Jay Carty, *Discovering Your Natural Talents* (Colorado Springs, CO: NavPress, 1994).

15. R. Paul Stevens, *The Other Six Days: Vocation, Work, and Ministry in Biblical Perspective* (Grand Rapids, MI: Eerdmans, 1999), 81-82.

16. Palmer, 25.

17. Gordon T. Smith, *Courage and Calling: Embracing Your God-Given Potential* (Downers Grove, IL: InterVarsity Press, 1999), 40.

18. Bruce Bugbee, *What You Do Best in the Body of Christ: Discover Your Spiritual Gifts, Personal Style, and God-Given Passion*, rev. ed. (Grand Rapids, MI: Zondervan, 2005), 82-86.

19. Douglas J. Schuurman, *Vocation: Discerning Our Callings in Life* (Grand Rapids, MI: Eerdmans, 2004), 142.

20. Miller and Hendricks, 66.

21. Gordon MacDonald, "God's Calling Plan," *Leadership* 24 (2003): 42.

22. Schuurman, 142, 63.
23. Lee Hardy, *The Fabric of This World: Inquiries into Calling, Career Choice, and the Design of Human Work* (Grand Rapids, MI: Eerdmans, 1990), 98.
24. Palmer, 49.
25. Gordon T. Smith, *Listening to God in Times of Choice: The Art of Discerning God's Will* (Downers Grove, IL: InterVarsity Press, 1997), 128.
26. Ray Kesner, "Vocational Discernment," in *Experiencing Ministry Supervision: A Field-Based Approach*, ed. William T. Pyle and Mary Alice Seals (Nashville: Broadman and Holman, 1995), 38.
27. David C. Ward, "Theological Archaeology: A Model for Theological Reflection in Field Education" (ThM thesis, Dallas Theological Seminary, 1998), 70.
28. Smith, *Listening to God*, 22.
29. David G. Benner, *The Gift of Being Yourself: The Sacred Call to Self-Discovery* (Downers Grove, IL: InterVarsity Press, 2004), 35.
30. Charles R. Swindoll, *The Mystery of God's Will: What Does He Want for Me?* (Nashville: Word Publishing, 1999), ix.
31. Benner, 40.

Chapter 3, What Are the Ingredients for a Healthy Internship?

1. Craig P. Donovan and Jim Garnett, *Internships for Dummies* (New York: Hungry Minds, 2001), 18, 292-94.
2. Malcolm S. Knowles, *The Modern Practice of Adult Education: From Pedagogy to Andragogy* (River Grove, IL: Follett, 1980).
3. Howard G. Hendricks and William D. Hendricks, *As Iron Sharpens Iron: Building Character in a Mentoring Relationship* (Chicago: Moody Press, 1995), 51-56.

4. Sharon Ting, "Our View of Coaching for Leadership Development," in *The CCL Handbook of Coaching: A Guide for the Leader Coach*, ed. Sharon Ting and Peter Scisco (San Francisco: Jossey-Bass, 2006), 17; Laura Whitworth, Henry Kimsey-House, and Phil Sandahl, *Co-Active Coaching: New Skills for Coaching People toward Success in Work and Life* (Palo Alto, CA: Davies-Black, 1998), 3-4.

5. As noted in the preface, I am using the word *mentor* to denote the on-site person who is responsible for the internship. Your school may use the term *supervisor* or *coach*. If your school uses another term for this on-site individual, please substitute that word as you read this book. Also, I know that individuals in addition to the mentor may be involved in providing oversight and direction during the internship. Some schools and denominations require the intern to have a lay committee, an advisory council, or ministry consultants on-site in addition to the mentor. If you are reading this book as a member of such a group, please understand that the qualities important for a mentor are also important for the members of this group. This group of individuals is a key component in the development of the intern.

6. Regina Coll, *Supervision of Ministry Students* (Collegeville, MN: The Liturgical Press, 1992), 16.

7. Keith R. Anderson and Randy D. Reese, *Spiritual Mentoring: A Guide for Seeking and Giving Direction* (Downers Grove, IL: InterVarsity Press, 1999), 17-18.

8. Lois J. Zachary, *The Mentor's Guide: Facilitating Effective Learning Relationships* (San Francisco: Jossey-Bass, 2000), 121.

9. Ting, 17-18.

10. Whitworth, Kimsey-House, and Sandahl, 32.

11. James D. Whitehead and Evelyn Eaton Whitehead, eds., *Method in Ministry: Theological Reflection and Christian*

Ministry, rev. ed. (Lanham, MD: Sheed & Ward, 1995), 69-70.

12. Whitworth, Kimsey-House, and Sandahl, 9, 15-18.
13. Ibid., 39.
14. Ting, 17.
15. Coll, 76.
16. Marian N. Ruderman and Patricia J. Ohlott, "Coaching Women Leaders," in Ting and Scisco, *The CCL Handbook of Coaching: A Guide for the Leader Coach*, 68.
17. Bobb Biehl, *Mentoring: Confidence in Finding a Mentor and Becoming One* (Nashville: Broadman and Holman, 1996), 65.
18. Ruderman and Ohlott, 82.
19. Ibid., 81.
20. Donovan and Garnett, 136.
21. Shalom H. Schwartz, "Cultural Value Differences: Some Implications for Work," *Applied Psychology: An International Review* 48 (1999): 33-34; Geert Hofstede, *Culture's Consequences: Comparing Values, Behaviors, Institutions, and Organizations across Nations* (Thousand Oaks, CA: Sage, 2001).
22. Lynne DeLay and Maxine Dalton, "Coaching across Cultures," in Ting and Scisco, *The CCL Handbook of Coaching: A Guide for the Leader Coach*, 146; Zachary, 41-47.
23. Saleem Assaf and Rosanne Lurie, *The Wetfeet Insider Guide to Getting Your Ideal Internship* (San Francisco: WetFeet, 2003), 13-14.

Chapter 4, What Are the Goals for Your Internship?

1. Stephen Graves and Thomas Addington, *A Case for Character: Authentic Living in Your Workplace* (Nashville: Broadman & Holman, 1998), xiii.

2. James M. Kouzes and Barry Z. Posner, *The Leadership Challenge,* 3rd ed., (San Francisco: Jossey-Bass, 2002), 24-27. The percentages listed are from their 2002 study.

3. Ibid., 27, 32.

4. Daniel Goleman, Richard Boyatzis, and Annie McKee, *Primal Leadership: Realizing the Power of Emotional Intelligence* (Boston: Harvard Business School Press, 2002); Cynthia D. McCauley and Ellen Van Velsor, eds., *The Center for Creative Leadership Handbook of Leadership Development* (San Francisco: Jossey-Bass, 2004); Andrew Seidel, *Charting a Bold Course: Training Leaders for 21st Century Ministry* (Chicago: Moody Press, 2003); Kouzes and Posner, *The Leadership Challenge,* 3rd ed.; Aubrey Malphurs, *Being Leaders: The Nature of Authentic Christian Leadership* (Grand Rapids, MI: Baker Books, 2003); Pyle and Seals, *Experiencing Ministry Supervision*; Warren Bennis and Burt Nanus, *Leaders: Strategies for Taking Charge,* 2nd ed. (New York: Collins, 2003); Marshall Sashkin and Molly G. Sashkin, *Leadership That Matters: The Critical Factors for Making a Difference in People's Lives and Organizations' Success* (San Francisco: Berrett-Koehler, 2003); Bernard M. Bass, *Bass and Stogdill's Handbook of Leadership: Theory, Research, and Managerial Applications,* 3rd ed. (New York: The Free Press, 1990); Daniel O. Aleshire et al., *Profiles of Ministry: Interpretive Manual Stage II,* rev. ed. (Pittsburgh: The Association of Theological Schools, 1999).

5. This list was developed over the years by the input of the faculty of Dallas Theological Seminary.

6. Sharon Ting and E. Wayne Hart, "Formal Coaching," in McCauley and Van Velsor, *The Center for Creative Leadership Handbook of Leadership Development,* 146.

7. Ibid., 147.

8. Ibid., 7.

9. James M. Kouzes and Barry Z. Posner, *The Leadership Challenge*, 2nd ed. (San Francisco: Jossey-Bass, 1995), 326-27.
10. Sharon Ting and Doug Riddle, "A Framework for Leadership Development Coaching," in Ting and Scisco, *The CCL Handbook of Coaching*, 46.
11. Ellen Van Velsor and Cynthia D. McCauley, "Our View of Leadership Development," in McCauley and Van Velsor, *The Center for Creative Leadership Handbook of Leadership Development*, 8-9.
12. Ibid., 8.
13. Ibid.
14. Ibid.
15. Ibid., 9.
16. Russ S. Moxley and Mary Lynn Pulley, "Hardships," in McCauley and Van Velsor, *The Center for Creative Leadership Handbook of Leadership Development*, 184.
17. Whitworth, Kimsey-House, and Sandahl, 157.
18. Ting and Riddle, "A Framework for Leadership Development Coaching," 47.
19. Ting and Hart, "Formal Coaching," 145.
20. Zachary, 25.

Chapter 5, What Did You Learn during Your Internship?

1. Kenneth H. Pohly, *Transforming the Rough Places: The Ministry of Supervision*, 2nd ed. (Franklin, TN: Providence House, 2001), 121.
2. Moxley and Pulley, 195.
3. Abigail Johnson, *Reflecting with God: Connecting Faith and Daily Life in Small Groups* (Herndon, VA: The Alban Institute, 2004), 105.
4. Moxley and Pulley, 195.

5. Morgan W. McCall, Michael M. Lombardo, and Ann M. Morrison, *The Lessons of Experience: How Successful Executives Develop on the Job* (New York: The Free Press, 1988), 87-94.

6. Kouzes and Posner, *The Leadership Challenge,* 3rd ed., 319.

7. Pohly, 121.

8. George I. Hunter, *Supervision and Education-Formation for Ministry* (Cambridge, MA: Episcopal Divinity School, 1982), 30.

9. Henry Cloud and John Townsend, *How People Grow: What the Bible Reveals about Personal Growth* (Grand Rapids, MI: Zondervan, 2001), 327.

10. Pohly, 86-87.

11. Craig T. Chappelow, "360-Degree Feedback," in McCauley and Van Velsor, *The Center for Creative Leadership Handbook of Leadership Development,* 63.

12. Mary Alice Seals, "Evaluation in the Supervisory Experience," in Pyle and Seals, *Experiencing Ministry Supervision,* 130-31.

13. Hunter, 61-62.

14. Johnson, 17.

15. William T. Pyle, "Theological Reflection," in Pyle and Seals, *Experiencing Ministry Supervision,* 111.

16. Johnson, 67.

17. Howard W. Stone and James O. Duke, *How to Think Theologically,* 2nd ed. (Minneapolis: Fortress Press, 2006), 43, 45.

18. Van Velsor and McCauley, "Our View of Leadership Development," 8-9.

19. Hunter, 88.

20. Daniel Goleman, *Emotional Intelligence: Why It Can Matter More Than IQ* (New York: Bantam Books, 1995), 43, 289-90.

21. Johnson, 64.
22. Patricia O'Connell Killen and John De Beer, *The Art of Theological Reflection* (New York: Crossroad, 1995), 27.
23. Johnson, 4.
24. Stone and Duke, 60.
25. Stanley J. Grenz and Roger E. Olson, *Who Needs Theology? An Invitation to the Study of God* (Downers Grove, IL: InterVarsity Press, 1996), 95.
26. Whitehead and Whitehead, 23.
27. Grenz and Olson, 96, 98.
28. Killen and De Beer, viii.
29. Whitehead and Whitehead, 5.
30. Center for Christian Leadership, *Identity-Investigating Who I Am*, ed. William G. Miller, Transforming Life Series (Richardson, TX: Biblical Studies Press, 2004), 44-46.
31. Whitehead and Whitehead, 56.
32. DeLay and Dalton, 125.
33. Whitehead and Whitehead, 53.
34. Center for Christian Leadership, 46.
35. Ibid., 46-47.
36. Patricia O'Connell Killen, "Assisting Adults to Think Theologically," in Whitehead and Whitehead, *Method in Ministry*, 109.
37. Howard G. Hendricks and William D. Hendricks, *Living by the Book* (Chicago: Moody Press, 1991), 283.

Epilogue, Playing in the Dirt

1. Carroll A. Wise, *Religion in Illness and Health* (New York: Harper and Brothers, 1942), 264.
2. R. Paul Stevens, *Down-to-Earth Spirituality: Encountering God in the Ordinary, Boring Stuff of Life* (Downers Grove, IL: InterVarsity Press, 2003), 184.

Bibliography

Aleshire, Daniel O., David S. Schuller, Dorothy L. Williams, and Francis A. Lonsway. *Profiles of Ministry: Interpretive Manual Stage II*. Rev. ed. Pittsburgh: The Association of Theological Schools, 1999.

Anderson, Keith R., and Randy D. Reese. *Spiritual Mentoring: A Guide for Seeking and Giving Direction*. Downers Grove, IL: InterVarsity Press, 1999.

Assaf, Saleem, and Rosanne Lurie. *The Wetfeet Insider Guide to Getting Your Ideal Internship*. San Francisco: WetFeet, 2003.

Badcock, Gary D. *The Way of Life: A Theology of Christian Vocation*. Grand Rapids, MI: Eerdmans, 1998.

Bass, Bernard M. *Bass and Stogdill's Handbook of Leadership: Theory, Research, and Managerial Applications*. 3rd ed. New York: The Free Press, 1990.

Benner, David G. *The Gift of Being Yourself: The Sacred Call to Self-Discovery*. Downers Grove, IL: InterVarsity Press, 2004.

Bennis, Warren, and Burt Nanus. *Leaders: Strategies for Taking Charge*. 2nd ed. New York: Collins, 2003.

Biehl, Bobb. *Mentoring: Confidence in Finding a Mentor and Becoming One*. Nashville: Broadman and Holman, 1996.

Buckingham, Marcus, and Donald O. Clifton. *Now, Discover Your Strengths*. New York: The Free Press, 2001.

Bugbee, Bruce. *What You Do Best in the Body of Christ: Discover Your Spiritual Gifts, Personal Style, and God-Given Passion.* Rev. ed. Grand Rapids, MI: Zondervan, 2005.

Center for Christian Leadership. *Identity—Investigating Who I Am.* Edited by William G. Miller, Transforming Life Series. Richardson, TX: Biblical Studies Press, 2004.

Chappelow, Craig T. "360-Degree Feedback." In *The Center for Creative Leadership Handbook of Leadership Development,* edited by Cynthia D. McCauley and Ellen Van Velsor, 58-84. San Francisco: Jossey-Bass, 2004.

Cloud, Henry, and John Townsend. *How People Grow: What the Bible Reveals about Personal Growth.* Grand Rapids, MI: Zondervan, 2001.

Coll, Regina. *Supervision of Ministry Students.* Collegeville, MN: The Liturgical Press, 1992.

DeLay, Lynne, and Maxine Dalton. "Coaching across Cultures." In *The CCL Handbook of Coaching: A Guide for the Leader Coach,* edited by Sharon Ting and Peter Scisco, 122-48. San Francisco: Jossey-Bass, 2006.

Donovan, Craig P., and Jim Garnett. *Internships for Dummies.* New York: Hungry Minds, 2001.

Goleman, Daniel. *Emotional Intelligence: Why It Can Matter More Than IQ.* New York: Bantam Books, 1995.

Goleman, Daniel, Richard Boyatzis, and Annie McKee. *Primal Leadership: Realizing the Power of Emotional Intelligence.* Boston: Harvard Business School Press, 2002.

Graves, Stephen, and Thomas Addington. *A Case for Character: Authentic Living in Your Workplace.* Nashville: Broadman & Holman, 1998.

Grenz, Stanley J., and Roger E. Olson. *Who Needs Theology? An Invitation to the Study of God.* Downers Grove, IL: InterVarsity Press, 1996.

Guinness, Os. *The Call: Finding and Fulfilling the Central Purpose of Your Life.* Nashville: W Publishing Group, 1998.

Hardy, Lee. *The Fabric of This World: Inquiries into Calling, Career Choice, and the Design of Human Work.* Grand Rapids, MI: Eerdmans, 1990.

Hendricks, Howard G., and William D. Hendricks. *As Iron Sharpens Iron: Building Character in a Mentoring Relationship.* Chicago: Moody Press, 1995.

————. *Living by the Book.* Chicago: Moody Press, 1991.

Hofstede, Geert. *Culture's Consequences: Comparing Values, Behaviors, Institutions, and Organizations across Nations.* Thousand Oaks, CA: Sage, 2001.

Hunter, George I. *Supervision and Education-Formation for Ministry.* Cambridge, MA: Episcopal Divinity School, 1982.

Johnson, Abigail. *Reflecting with God: Connecting Faith and Daily Life in Small Groups.* Herndon, VA: The Alban Institute, 2004.

Kesner, Ray. "Vocational Discernment." In *Experiencing Ministry Supervision: A Field-Based Approach,* edited by William T. Pyle and Mary Alice Seals. Nashville: Broadman and Holman, 1995.

Killen, Patricia O'Connell. "Assisting Adults to Think Theologically." In *Method in Ministry: Theological Reflection and Christian Ministry,* edited by James D. Whitehead and Evelyn Eaton Whitehead, 103-11. Lanham, MD: Sheed & Ward, 1995.

Killen, Patricia O'Connell, and John De Beer. *The Art of Theological Reflection.* New York: Crossroad, 1995.

Knowles, Malcolm S. *The Modern Practice of Adult Education: From Pedagogy to Andragogy.* River Grove, IL: Follett, 1980.

Kouzes, James M., and Barry Z. Posner. *The Leadership Challenge.* 2nd ed. San Francisco: Jossey-Bass, 1995.

————. *The Leadership Challenge.* 3rd ed. San Francisco: Jossey-Bass, 2002.

Lonsway, Francis A. *The Graduating Student Questionnaire: A Study of Five Years of Use 1996-1997 through 2000-2001.* Pittsburgh: The Association of Theological Schools, 2002.

Luther, Martin. "Sunday After Christmas, Luke 2:33-40." In *The Precious and Sacred Writings of Martin Luther*. Edited by John Nicholas Lenker. Minneapolis: Lutherans in All Lands, 1905, 10:255-307.

MacDonald, Gordon. "God's Calling Plan." *Leadership* 24 (2003): 35-42.

Malphurs, Aubrey. *Being Leaders: The Nature of Authentic Christian Leadership*. Grand Rapids: Baker Books, 2003.

McCall, Morgan W., Michael M. Lombardo, and Ann M. Morrison. *The Lessons of Experience: How Successful Executives Develop on the Job*. New York: The Free Press, 1988.

McCauley, Cynthia D., and Ellen Van Velsor, eds. *The Center for Creative Leadership Handbook of Leadership Development*. San Francisco: Jossey-Bass, 2004.

Miller, Arthur F., Jr., and William D. Hendricks. *The Power of Uniqueness: How to Become Who You Really Are*. Grand Rapids, MI: Zondervan, 1999.

Moxley, Russ S., and Mary Lynn Pulley. "Hardships." In *The Center for Creative Leadership Handbook of Leadership Development*, edited by Cynthia D. McCauley and Ellen Van Velsor. San Francisco: Jossey-Bass, 2004.

Palmer, Parker J. *Let Your Life Speak: Listening for the Voice of Vocation*. San Francisco: Jossey-Bass, 2000.

Placher, William C., ed. *Callings: Twenty Centuries of Christian Wisdom on Vocation*. Grand Rapids: Eerdmans, 2005.

Pohly, Kenneth H. *Transforming the Rough Places: The Ministry of Supervision*. 2nd ed. Franklin, TN: Providence House, 2001.

Pyle, William T. "Theological Reflection." In *Experiencing Ministry Supervision*, edited by William T. Pyle and Mary Alice Seals, 109-24. Nashville: Broadman and Holman, 1995.

Pyle, William T., and Mary Alice Seals, eds. *Experiencing Ministry Supervision: A Field-Based Approach*. Nashville: Broadman and Holman, 1995.

Ruderman, Marian N., and Patricia J. Ohlott. "Coaching Women Leaders." In *The CCL Handbook of Coaching: A Guide for the Leader Coach*, edited by Sharon Ting and Peter Scisco, 65-91. San Francisco: Jossey-Bass, 2006.

Sashkin, Marshall, and Molly G. Sashkin. *Leadership That Matters: The Critical Factors for Making a Difference in People's Lives and Organizations' Success*. San Francisco: Berrett-Koehler, 2003.

Schuurman, Douglas J. *Vocation: Discerning Our Callings in Life*. Grand Rapids, MI: Eerdmans, 2004.

Schwartz, Shalom H. "Cultural Value Differences: Some Implications for Work." *Applied Psychology: An International Review* 48 (1999): 23-48.

Schwehn, Mark R., and Dorothy C. Bass. *Leading Lives That Matter: What We Should Do and Who We Should Be*. Grand Rapids: Eerdmans, 2006.

Seals, Mary Alice. "Evaluation in the Supervisory Experience." In *Experiencing Ministry Supervision: A Field-Based Approach*, edited by William T. Pyle and Mary Alice Seals, 125-37. Nashville: Broadman and Holman, 1995.

Seidel, Andrew. *Charting a Bold Course: Training Leaders for 21st Century Ministry*. Chicago: Moody Press, 2003.

Smith, Gordon T. *Courage and Calling: Embracing Your God-Given Potential*. Downers Grove, IL: InterVarsity Press, 1999.

———. *Listening to God in Times of Choice: The Art of Discerning God's Will*. Downers Grove, IL: InterVarsity Press, 1997.

Stevens, R. Paul. *Down-to-Earth Spirituality: Encountering God in the Ordinary, Boring Stuff of Life*. Downers Grove, IL: Inter-Varsity Press, 2003.

———. *The Other Six Days: Vocation, Work, and Ministry in Biblical Perspective*. Grand Rapids: Eerdmans, 1999.

Stone, Howard W., and James O. Duke. *How to Think Theologically*. 2nd ed. Minneapolis: Fortress Press, 2006.

Swindoll, Charles R. *The Mystery of God's Will: What Does He Want for Me?* Nashville: Word Publishing, 1999.

Ting, Sharon. "Our View of Coaching for Leadership Development." In *The CCL Handbook of Coaching: A Guide for the Leader Coach*, edited by Sharon Ting and Peter Scisco, 15-33. San Francisco: Jossey-Bass, 2006.

Ting, Sharon, and E. Wayne Hart. "Formal Coaching." In *The Center for Creative Leadership Handbook of Leadership Development*, edited by Cynthia D. McCauley and Ellen Van Velsor. San Francisco: Jossey-Bass, 2004.

Ting, Sharon, and Doug Riddle. "A Framework for Leadership Development Coaching." In *The CCL Handbook of Coaching: A Guide for the Leader Coach*, edited by Sharon Ting and Peter Scisco, 34-62. San Francisco: Jossey-Bass, 2006.

Van Velsor, Ellen, and Cynthia D. McCauley. "Our View of Leadership Development." In *The Center for Creative Leadership Handbook of Leadership Development*, edited by Cynthia D. McCauley and Ellen Van Velsor, 1-22. San Francisco: Jossey-Bass, 2004.

Ward, David C. "Theological Archaeology: A Model for Theological Reflection in Field Education." ThM thesis, Dallas Theological Seminary, 1998.

Whitehead, James D., and Evelyn Eaton Whitehead. *Method in Ministry: Theological Reflection and Christian Ministry*. Rev. ed. Lanham, MD: Sheed & Ward, 1995.

Whitworth, Laura, Henry Kimsey-House, and Phil Sandahl. *Co-Active Coaching: New Skills for Coaching People toward Success in Work and Life*. Palo Alto, CA: Davies-Black, 1998.

Wise, Carroll A. *Religion in Illness and Health*. New York: Harper and Brothers, 1942.

Zachary, Lois J. *The Mentor's Guide: Facilitating Effective Learning Relationships*. San Francisco: Jossey-Bass, 2000.